Beauty and The Bastard

Beauty and The Bastard

JOHN THOMAS

John Thomas
Beauty and The Bastard

This book is a work of fiction. Names, characters, places, and incidents are products of the author's imagination or are used fictitiously. Any resemblance to actual persons, living or dead, events, or locales is purely coincidental.

Published by Spines Publishing Platform
ISBN: 979-8-89569-990-4

Dedication

This book is a heartfelt tribute to those who have journeyed through my life, whether as a guiding light or a formidable challenge. To my beloved children, you are the essence of my existence; it is your laughter and dreams that ignite my perseverance when the weight of the world seems overwhelming. While I can't promise to hold you for the rest of your lives, I vow to love you fiercely for all of mine.

To my mother, in reflection, though I didn't see the formidable struggles you faced raising three sons at such a tender age, juggling the quest for acceptance, self-love and identity amidst chaos. Though devoid of a roadmap, you forged onward, and for that, I offer forgiveness and understanding.

To my grandmother Barbra, I extend forgiveness as well. I have come to realize that history has a relentless cadence, repeating itself with or without cause until its cycle is broken. Each day, as I am greeted by the radiant smiles of my children, I wish you were here to share in that joy.

To all my siblings, both maternal and paternal, my heart brims with love for you all, now and always.

And finally, to life itself: you have unrelentingly hurled me against rugged cliffs, tested me with trials that seemed insurmountable leaving me prostrated in valleys of despair bringing me to the brink of surrender where even death seemed a haven. Yet, inexplicably, I rise again and again, finding strength anew in the depths of my struggles.

Interlude

THE STORY OF MY LIFE: MACHELLA POWELL

At the tender age of 14, as I stepped into adolescence, I was enveloped by the profound uncertainty of impending motherhood. At 15, my firstborn, Steven, entered my life under truly extraordinary circumstances. His arrival was remarkable due to an unusual phenomenon, he was born with teeth. This bewildered and unnerved me, as it was beyond my knowledge that newborns could possess such traits. A hospital nurse calmed my concerns, assuring me that the teeth would naturally shed. Remarkably, the improbable occurred when Steven reached the age of two, as one tooth indeed fell out, turning this extraordinary event into a newspaper headline.

Two years later, I welcomed my second child, Antonio, into the world. Antonio, who was blessed with 12 fingers, presented another unexpected challenge. Once again, the nurses comforted me, predicting the natural loss of these extra digits. True to their word, the fingers eventually detached, allowing what seemed like the beginning of an ordinary life.

Lacking consistent maternal guidance, I was compelled to mature rapidly. My mother, preoccupied with her own ventures, was seldom present. In her absence, my Uncle James, affectionately known as Hook, became my mentor in his small one-bedroom apartment, where I resided with my three siblings and two children. Despite feeling grown-up, I was confused and struggling, trying to piece together what it meant to be both a parent and an individual. As a kid myself raising kids, finding self-love and identity was a monumental challenge. I often felt lost.

Two more years elapsed before my third son, John, arrived free from any birth anomalies. Yet, our relief was short-lived as John soon fell gravely ill, suffering relentless vomiting and diarrhea. In desperation, I turned to my mother, leading us to the emergency room. There, we discovered his severe dehydration, a situation that, tragically, attracted Child Protective Services into our lives. Their intervention resulted in John's removal from my care, a searing three-month ordeal, until I was vindicated and joyfully reunited with him.

As time unfolded, a close relative introduced me to cocaine, beginning a tumultuous phase marked by personal battles and mistakes. I allowed drugs to become my escape from a world I perceived as unjust. Despite my efforts to nurture my sons, the love I lacked from my own mother hindered my ability to do so fully. Although well-meaning, my father was frequently absent. Legal complications led to a stint in prison ultimately from 1990-96, and leaving my children ages 3, 5 and 7 under my mother's care proved disastrous, as my boys suffered physical, verbal, and mental abuse at her hands. Heartbreakingly, my youngest son John suffered a near-fatal accident after being struck by a truck while retrieving mail. By divine mercy, his life was spared, though the incident devastated me.

In my desperation to provide for my children, is how I found myself incarcerated. I had watched a close relative exploit the system through larceny, witnessing their apparent success, which misguidedly gave me the impression that such actions could ensure a better life for my sons. Naively following in their footsteps led to my arrest, costing me years of my life in prison and separating me from the very children I sought to support.

As a mother striving to navigate life without any understanding or direction, I feel I failed my boys. This is a part of me I cannot reclaim. However, I have made peace with it and built relationships with my sons, though, regrettably, all three encountered issues with the law. Two of them entered the penitentiary, with John forfeiting ten years of freedom from the age of 16. Yet, my son emerged from prison neither bitter nor institutionalized, finding light amidst those dark times.

Today, I am blessed with the joy of 13 grandchildren and one great-grandchild. Reflecting on my turbulent journey, I remain grateful to God for shaping me into the woman and grandmother I am today. I am committed to continual learning. Despite the trials, my faith remains steadfast, enriching my life with immeasurable happiness.

I am indebted to my son for allowing me to share this tapestry of my life. The tribulations faced and the lessons learned have left indelible marks on them. However, as a parent acknowledging my mistakes, I wish to impart this wisdom: it is never too late to make amends. Through God, all things are possible. Enjoy.

PROUD OF THAT TOOTH: Three-week-old Steven Earl Junior Johnson opens wide to show off tiny tooth as he is cuddled by maternal grandmother, Barbara Johnson, 30, (left) and mother, Machelle Johnson, 14. Miss Johnson, a freshman at Benton Harbor High School, said tooth was growing in her son's mouth when he was born at Memorial Hospital Oct. 5. She said nurses told her tooth would fall out after couple weeks, "but it hasn't and it keeps getting bigger." Miss Johnson and her mother live in Blossom Acres housing project, Concord Road, Benton Township. (Staff photo by John Madill)

Contents

Beauty and the Bastard is a unique poetry manuscript made up of spoken words, life and inspiration. These poems goes deep inside the mind of a poet's experiences, imagination, life and creativity.

Question

Like so many others, I dream of wealth beyond imagination, millions and billions of dollars an ocean of riches flowing into my life. I envision mini mansions adorned with extravagance, sleek foreign cars gliding through sunlit streets, and an endless supply of luxuries, the finer things that life has to offer. Yet, as I immerse myself in these fantasies, I pause to ponder: why? Life isn't a game that can be won with riches. What is the point of escaping struggles if we still confront emotional and moral difficulties within ourselves?

Money may place you on a higher pedestal, but it can never truly define who you are. It can't rewrite the past, amend wrongs, nor can it extract joy from the essence of pain. Love, that invaluable treasure, is often tainted by the shadows of wealth; it can sabotage relationships rather than nurture them.

Too often, lives are lost in the pursuit of mere pocket change, a tragic toll for fleeting gains. True peace and happiness remain elusive, slipping through our fingers no matter the fortune amassed. It leaves us to ponder the underlying question: why do we hold these pieces of paper in such high regard? What is it we seek in the wealth we aspire to attain? The harsh reality is that all money can truly buy is status and a fleeting sense of self-esteem, leaving the more profound desires of the heart untouched and unfulfilled.

A Call to Revive Hip-Hop's Heart and Soul

Music used to be therapeutic,
A real substance in rap, I remember.
Knowledge was being pushed to us,
Nowadays these rappers is dope fiends.
It went from talkin' 'bout the struggle, having and not having,
Inspiration with hopes that someday you'll live the American dream to lyrical content devoted to molly, percocet, promethazine.
It's a shame how the game lost its gleam.
Once a beacon of hope, now a sad, hollow scene.
We used to rise with the message, now we fall to the beat, chasing highs losing touch with the real streets.
Gone are the days of Public Enemy's fight.
Now we just chase the bag, and lose sight of the light.
Where's the revolution, the fire, the truth?
We traded our wisdom for a fountain of youth.

I remember Nas teaching me about the world outside. Now it's all about the drip, the car, the ride.
The depth's been replaced by a shallow display,
we glorify the vices, push the virtues away.
Once we were kings, now we follow trends,
It's time to reclaim the message and make amends.
Let's bring back the days of lyrical finesse,
Where the words had weight, and the beats impressed.
From the cyphers on the corner to the stages bright,
we need to resurrect the soul, bring back the light.
Hip-hop's more than a party, it's a voice and a dream, it's atestament to the struggle, a vision, and a theme.
I long for the era of the conscious rhyme,
when every bar was a lesson, every verse a sign.
From Rakim to KRS, they set the stage,
we need a renaissance, a turn of the page.
Let's lift the veil, expose the real scene,
Reclaim the crown, and restore the dream.

A Child's Cry for Love in a World of Neglect

All the years of neglect you seem surprised to be where we are now? Not once have you ever tried to lift me up. The reverse psychology doesn't work for a child so the negative things you said you may have thought would make me turn my act around but in all reality what I really needed was a hug, the things you used to say only put me down. Bottled up emotionally locked away scared to let go in fear of not being found. What I found was an abandoned car to live in when you put me out without a place to go. It was winter so the nights were cold when I was 14 years old. How many times can you recall showing up for me never not once not at all your only concern was with whom you were involved like a chain smoker and men were your menthol. You put a bunch of men before us funny because the bible will teach you that Eve was Adam's downfall. You couldn't differentiate the two so you chose men and threw us to the lions in the zoo. You let my brother your son rot in jail but made sure a man you have no relation with to this day make bail.

Do you remember the time you made me and my brother pull a drug dealer off the street into our home and confront him about a crack sale, Tonio ran away that very same day guess what mama he picked up crack to sell. You treated us like shit believe it or not me and Steve followed in your footsteps by going off to prison while your second to oldest boy could have lost his life behind getting shot. Grandmama used to abuse us simply for things we didn't know sometimes because her demons were in control meaning we got beat out of our sleep as a kid have you ever tried to sleep with only one eye closed. She used to tell us things like don't come down stairs and what she'd do if we'd roam so when we'd miss school we'd be punished as if we were to blame for doing something wrong in reality we'd yell and yell and yell but often times she was intoxicated so in her drunken state she couldn't hear us and by the time we made it to the stop that school bus was gone making that a dreadful walk home. We lived in the projects so when we'd wet the bed grandmama used to make us stand out in the blazing sun for all to see those same underwear we wore on our head. Her method was to embarrass us when she could have taught us instead. The Riddler you never knew who she was one minute she was medusa the next it was compassion and love her choice of music was rather unique, she had bunions so I never learned to slow dance when she tried to teach in fear of stepping on her feet. She sometimes held us close and told us she loved us. The duration didn't matter, she still did it. I can't count how many times you expressed you loved us outside of the prison phone. One hug is all I can remember most of my childhood life and that's the day you came home. but I forgive you somehow, mama did you really love me or was I just a child?

A Heart Shaped by Struggle

I feel as though I possess no heart, shaped by the wounds and trials of this life. Smiles are few and far between; my childhood has left a lasting impact on my mind. While I'm not a menace to society, my reflections have occasionally resonated with those of Kane. The question of whether I live or die is one I simply cannot answer. I'm ensnared in a world where color continues to be a dividing line. Being Black in America means grappling with struggle, hustling to survive, or facing the harsh reality of death.

As a child of the ghetto, I refuse to be victimized by the blindness around me. "We must take a stand; we're fighting to survive," are the words that resonate from my own people. Yet, from the outside, I see not a fight for peace of mind but rather a pursuit of material wealth—empty gains that won't follow us when it's time to transcend.

Pain doesn't stem from the heart; it invades my thoughts like termites consuming wood, leaving agony in its wake. Inside me lie memories darker than demise itself. The ink is my tears, these lines is the earth they fall upon when my soul cry. I don't harbor hatred for you or him; it's the neglect that my conscience has grown to detest.

Born in '87, that year marked the beginning of a curse —a gift that brought me to this hell on earth.

A Hearts Plea for Redemption

I'm not trying to change anything that's happened. The only change I can make is within myself—how I treat you, how I look at and speak to you. I want to find peace and humility with you, to build a family with you. What I've done over the years can't be changed or erased, but I long for your heart in return for your belief that I won't walk away. If I could have one thing, it would be your love, locked inside a cave, so that when I die, your love will follow me to the grave.

For six years, I've been going through a phase. I was an adult physically, but mentally, I was not of age, trapped in my own thoughts. I was a slave to everything that eventually led me astray. There's a difference between love and attention, between women and fleeting encounters, between beginnings and endings. I used to love the attention from others, but now that I've come to my senses and want to right my wrongs, it feels like your love for me is fading.

I remember when you asked me, “Can you write a poem about me?” I said yes, but I didn’t really know how or what to say. My thoughts were so cluttered with all the things I wanted to express that I was unsure about the right words. Sometimes, saying “I love you” is enough, but it means nothing if your actions tell a different story. My love for you is like that grass stain you could never wash away—it's here to stay, just like a fat kid loves cake.

That’s not my style; I’m not just trying to say anything to make you smile. The truth is, all of this should have been said a long time ago. I know I’ve lost you, but somehow I’m still in denial. You’re the one who’s hurt, so why am I the one shedding tears? I’ve cried so much lately that if I were precipitation in the sky, people in the world would despise me. I cry because, as a man, I’ve come to accept my wrongs—a process that has taken far too long because that love I desperately desire is gone.

I cry because I feel sad, hurt, and alone. I never knew I could feel such pain from causing pain to others. Now I understand how it feels to lose someone you love, and it makes it hard to carry on. I cry because, as a man with many poor decisions, I’m constantly reminded of my past actions, even as I pursue change. This change didn’t come overnight; it took for that little voice in my head to climb the stairs to my mind and turn on the light, showing me that the way I was living wasn’t right. Now, as I strive to do better, love has walked out of my life, packed its bags and left.

I cry because I never intended for things to end up this way. I cry because I was given more than enough chances to get it right, but somewhere inside, my mind wasn’t where it needed to be until it was finally exposed to the light. I cry because I want to give love and receive love until the end of our lives together. I cry because you've moved on when I should have been the one you love the most. I cry because it's eating me alive to know that someone else is holding you close at night. I cry because I love you, and if that's wrong, then I don't want to be right

A Journey Through Pain, Paradox, and Pursuit of Justice

Walk with me on a journey through my uncharted division where "protect and serve" has turned into rogue missions. Kill em all it seems that's the message they've been told—

Who are "they"? The black lives, their stories unfold. Just the other day, I saw footage so cold, a cop pinned a black kid with a speeding truck, as the teen fled, running for his life.

They're killing us, and these are the same folks
We're supposed to call upon to save the day.

Nah, what I really want to do will get me locked in a cell or worse, fading away.

I wonder why I feel nonchalant, Harboring hate for cops to this day.

Blue lives matter? Nah, we all bleed the same;
When it splatters, it's all red, no one can be blamed.
It's laughter until a cop's daughter, son, or wife
becomes a victim of the massacre of life.

Touch one of mine, it's only right you lose one of yours.

Many racist cops are living by that code,

so it's a must you die by the sword or die from a shot from a SIG or a Glock from a kid on the block, sittin' in that cop car you ain't see 'em comin' too late, eight shots have your body numbing' or die with a knife six inches in the head I could die on death row, sentenced to the chair.

A Journey Through the Darkness

In a cell where shadows draped my soul,
with holy texts, my only sky and goal,
confusion wrapped around my fragile heart,
at sixteen, lost and torn apart. A holy Quran
and Bible by my side, I prayed to whispers
beyond the divide. Whoever answered first
would guide my way, in the silence where
my spirit lay. My time hadn't yet begun its
flight, yet I felt buried beneath the night.
The weight of earth upon my chest,
in a coffin of despair, seeking rest. Letters
absent, hope grew thin, no visits to remind
me of kin.
No voice to reach across the line, familiar faces
made their way to the exit sign inside my
mind, loneliness, a friend in every rhyme.
Each prayer a tether to the stars, guidin' light
through prison bars.
In solitude, I found a spark, in faith a flame to

pierce the dark. For even trapped in walls so tight,
the soul finds ways to take flight. In sacred words I found my song, An inner strength that kept me strong. So here's to battles fought with grace,
and findin' hope in the darkest place. In silent prayers, my voice was heard, in faith and strength, my spirit stirred.

A Leaf's Legacy in the Winds of Time

We arrive in this world alone, and we depart in solitude, drifting quietly into the ether like whispers carried off by the wind. I am a solitary leaf, still clinging to the branches of my family tree, yet to be swept away by life's relentless currents. As autumn approaches, may the wisdom and strength I hold within resonate long after I'm gone, and may my legacy endure, etching itself into the fabric of eternity.

A Letter to the Lost Art of Hip-Hop

Once upon a time in the land of rhyme,
where the beats would thump, and the words would chime. 2Pac and Biggie, legends, you set the bar high,
but nowadays in the game, the truth it's a lie.
In a world so crass, where the bars don't matter,
where rats clean the streets, and the truth's gone flatter, lyrical depth traded for flash and for clout,
but hear me out, that's not what it's about.
Biggie, what's this I hear? Puff's in the pen, we remember the years, Diddy took risks, now he's facing his fears, from the Bad Boy days, to the life he led, but tracks that were golden, are now filled with dread, a cell in the dark, the king of the shenanigans, left without a spark.
Pac, I was right there, listening close when you

whispered, "Suge shot me," on that
Makaveli album, a battle cry bold, but now
Suge's in chains, his empire on hold.
Keefe D, he claims he's the one with the gun,
but deep in the streets, no matter who's the
shooter that burdened still weighs a ton.
Yet we vibe to your tracks, feel your spirit alive,
in the echoes of the concrete, where the legends
thrive.
Jay-Z's at the top, he's still spitting fire,
fifty-plus chapters, he's never retired, dude still
runnin' the game, you should've heard'em
on, "God Did" Big he put the f in the defin-
ition of flame, with rhymes relentless, like a
beast on the prowl, when that needle drops,
he's the king, pure growl.
But the essence is fading, where's the lyrical
art?
Just auto tune vibes, no joy in the heart.
Yet in the shadows, a voice is gone unheard,
Mysonne's lyrical assassin, wisdom-rich and
absurd, but the radio waves just keep on
trespassing, they drown out the real and
push the truth to the back, while catchy
tunes mask the heart of a track. The
industry clamors for manufactured tales,
real talk gets eclipsed, a cruel path that it
trails.
Nas, still spittin' that raw, bringing heat to the
mic dismantling every flaw, but we sittin'
here watchin' with Kings Disease, a
struggle for the crown when we just wanna
breathe.

*Why'd it come to this? What happened to the
craft?
Where fire burned vibrant, with a lyrical
draft,
now gimmicks hold sway, the culture wears
thin,
but I'm clutching the memories, the legends
within.
Pac and Big, thank you for lighting the way
even in the chaos your words still relay, a
message of power and strength, through
darkness we roam, we carry your legacy,
you're forever at home.
In a world gone astray, with storytellers lost,
true writers rise from the ashes, no matter the
cost,
so let the beat thump, and the truth unfold,
for the spirit of the legends can never decline.
So I write this letter, in your honor I flow,
to the legends before us, did you know that we
know? The game is a circus, but your
legacy is strong. In a world full of chaos,
we'll keep singing your songs.*

A Reflection on Trust and Betrayal

Many of Dark Knight's depression has had me feeling like Heath Ledger reminiscin' thinking back on how family can betray you, have you on some nutty stuff with no correlations to the professor, those who warn you to watch the company you keep might be the same ones schemin' against you. Nowadays, it's wiser to keep things to yourself, it's often those you call family, not enemies, who pose the greatest threat, wearin' deceptive facades like wolves in sheep's cloth. They assume blood ties excuse them from respectin' principles' or any g-code. But they can be identified if you observe closely; deceitful people sometimes disguise themselves like officers in plainclothes.

That's why I maneuver with an Ill Mind like Hopsin. If you do too much for someone, they might become entitled, and as soon as you set boundaries, their betrayal starts. Although quietly observing, they are aware of your strengths. When you're cornered, you must either fold or make your move, like the iconic '97 pass to John Stockton. I'm like Chris Paul, always ready to act decisively, whether it's with a Clipper or a Rocket...

Adolescence

In order to judge me, you must delve into the depths of my story. To truly understand my journey, you need to grasp the roots from which I sprang, and to fathom where I come from, you must step into the very shoes I've worn... the shoes of my Adolescence.

My childhood unfolded in the shadow of my mother's imprisonment. While the walls closed around her, she sent letters and cards from behind bars, but I quickly learned that loving someone locked away is different from loving them in the freedom of the world. When she returned, that bond of affection faded like a ghost. My mother, who once sent me words of warmth, soon succumbed to a cycle of disenchantment, enamored by men who had little to offer echoing, in a painful parallel, the struggle of Black Americans in a world that seemed to cast them aside. She treated us like we were insignificant, just another detail lost in a system that failed to recognize our worth.

And then there was my father, a figure shrouded in mystery. Some claimed he was a good man, but through the eyes of my youthful perception, he was nothing but the specter of Sebastian Caine, a Hollow Man. I was aware of his existence, but he was a mere wisp in my reality, a stranger to the physical realm of my life a drop-dead Fred when responsibility beckoned. Seven other siblings existed in my periphery, but like shadows dancing on the walls of my life, they remained largely unknown to me.

My upbringing was shaped by an abusive alcoholic grandmother, a woman of unpredictable temper. One moment she held me in her loving embrace; the next, I'd be jolted awake from sleep, the stinging hand of her frustration teaching me fear rather than comfort. I lived paralyzed, unsure of which version of her would greet me each day, feeling akin to Kunta Kinte, lost and yearning for freedom. My brothers had families on their father's side, a refuge I did not possess. Alone, I faced the isolation of my own reality, while they were absorbed in their separate lives.

Though everyone adored her, my grandmother was not always cruel. The only person in my life brave enough to speak the truth, she dispensed wisdom harsh enough to choke upon, but it was her way unvarnished and raw. She took us in when our mothers dropped us off at strange family gatherings, often entrusting us to men who dared to mistreat us in their homes. When confronted, her retort was chillingly dismissive: "I was just brushing his head." And yet, in between those dark moments, she would hold us close, swaying gently to the smooth sounds of Al Green, tears streaming down her face like a cathartic rainstorm.

I remember the taste of E&J, the sharp burn that seared down my throat as she insisted we drink. In those fleeting moments, I thought of firefighters battling an inferno; they could never extinguish the flames igniting in the depths of my being, leaving an indelible mark. Raised in the projects, my grandmother forged me in the fires of struggle, teaching me to stand tall and fight like a man. The clatter of dice in her palm was my first lesson in counting, a makeshift education in a world that seemed to offer so little.

An Absent Minds Struggle

A black hole swallows me, aimless I glide,
into the abyss where shadows reside.
Not a dream, but a truth, I'm awake in this
plight,
plummetin' downward, consumed by the
night.
No winds lift my spirit, no tales to recall,
Just echoes of silence where memories fall.
No laughter, no joy, just a body in flight,
racing through darkness, like lightnin' when it
strikes.
And all that I yearn for, is nothin' at all.
How can I hope when to dream I've
withdrawn?
In the wilds of despair, how can a voice ring,
If I choose not to scream, if I let silence cling?
With no plans to escape, lost in the fray,
is there light for tomorrow, or will it all fade
away?

Born into the struggle, in isolation I dwell,
just another statistic in a personal hell.
The blind lead the blind, in shadows they
roam,
a hollow reflection of lost hopes and home.
The strife of the absent, a mind left behind.
In the void of existence, what solace can I find?
The struggle of an absent mind.

An Anthem of Hope Amidst the Storm

To exist in this world we must contend with
humiliation, broken dreams, sadness, and
loss,
navigatin' life's storms, searchin' for bridges to
cross. We rise from the ashes, each day a
new fight in a world where the strong often
prey on the slight.
Hope is a fragile thread we grasp in the night
clingin' to visions of a future that's bright.
Climbin' through the storm with fire in my
eyes,
no limit to my journey, determined to reach
where the eagle flies.
Educations neglected, their potential confined,
by the chains of a system that's callous and
blind.
The weight of oppression, a burden so deep,
in the hearts of the weary, it's a promise to
keep.

Through the haze of despair, we find ways to cope,
in the melodies of freedom, in the anthems of hope.
Art as our weapon, words as our shield, in the struggle for dignity, we refuse to yield.
Some of us paint our pain on the canvas of time. I structure mines in rhythms of rhyme.
The world may ignore us, but never will it be able to shut you out when you know your worth. In the depths of sorrow, I've found rebirth.
In the face of the storm I remain resolute,
heart beatin' steady to a timeless pursuit.
They don't think you hurt, no, they think you're immune, because you don't cry when in pain, you just keep licking the wounds..

Attentions the new currency

Greed used to be the sin leading people to their demise now it's attention, the captions and likes got us tangled in lies.
Chasin' follows, tradin' self-worth for validation as if it'll manifest into fame. It's a cold game.
Addicted to the screen unbeknownst, reality's eclipsed.
We crave the spotlight, but at what cost?
In the quest for clout, our true selves are lost.
Social media platforms have us all in chains, attention's the new currency, everyone's a slave.

Beauty in the Sand

When I'm enveloped in sadness, she appears like a radiant burst of sunshine, showering me with a thousand smiles freely bestowed. In my dreams, she dances through the shadows, weaving the fabric of her existence into the very essence of my slumber. The sun's warm embrace mirrors the vibrant fire of her identity, yet her name lingers on the tip of my tongue—an enchanting enigma.

At times, we clasp our hands together, lost in the depths of each other's gaze; at other moments, the gentle grace of her fingers caresses my cheek, enveloping me in the velvety softness of her touch. She has pressed her lips to my forehead countless times, imbuing each kiss with unwavering strength and hopeful whispers, wrapped in concern and tender care. Her glossy eyes, imbued with a beauty that defies description, draw me deeper into the ocean of her soul with every stolen glance.

In a haunting rhythm, she allows a single tear to escape, cradling it like a fragile jewel in her hands, holding it close to her heart in shared despair. For she knows, perhaps better than I, the fleeting moments before I'm drawn back to reality, summoned from my peaceful slumber. Then, with a bittersweet farewell, she blows me a kiss, gradually fading away, merging seamlessly with the white sandy beach.

Will I ever uncover her in the waking world, or is she merely an elusive mirage, a figment of my yearning heart that will forever remain out of reach?

Beyond the Concrete:

A CRY FOR UNITY IN A WORLD OF LIES

I transcend mere rhymes, I go beyond lines. I bear a reality that can't be captured through mere mortals' eyes—damn, ain't you exhausted by the web of lies? the shit that got me mortified my only wish is that more defy

In this concrete jungle, I've morphed into a beast; roots buried deep where fathers vanished before you took your first breath while mothers lost their grip, minds drifting into despair. The days of nurturing and teaching have faded like a stolen memory, so when you finally make it, nobody whispers, "I see you, keep climbing." First, they adore you, then that affection warps into disdain, a twisted transformation fueled by the greed of a dollar bill—families fracture, turning into cold shadows over checks.

I hail from a place where respect is worth dying for, not survival. Countless brands have tarnished our image, and yet we rally behind everything except our own—gravitating toward Tommy, Old Navy, or even Gucci. None of that sends a spark through my veins. We clamor for reparations, only to funnel our hopes right back into pockets that don't hold us dear or give a damn.

I'm rooted in a world where we battle, steal from, and extinguish our own kin, where the bloodshed flows freely when the conflict is us against us. The hatred runs deep, an inherited poison that seeps through our very beings. I come from a land where unity costs nothing, yet our programming whispers the lie that we must walk alone. When the sirens wail, we rush to the streets and unleash chaos.

Old heads didn't drop wisdom; they showed us how to slide like a playground,

never teaching us to invest our bread. A face plastered on a tee is how we respect the dead.

Black boy / White boy

They called the black boy foolish, eliciting the white boy's sneer. His dreams come without obstacles, while the black boy's path is unclear.
The white boy, cloaked in privilege, feels no racial sting, while the black boy confronts a world where discrimination is king.
Turn on the TV screen, hear a Klansman's vile decree, proclaiming white superiority, enforcing black inferiority.
The white boy reveres Hitler's destruction as his game. Columbus is falsely glorified, though history bears his shame.
Yet the black boy draws courage from leaders fierce and wise, 2Pac, Douglass, Newton, King Jr., their legacies on the rise.
An unarmed black boy stands as the white boy's weapon fires, his innocent life taken, a victim of racial desires.

Consider Plaxico's fate, punished harshly for his
plight, while Zimmerman walks free,
justice obscured from sight.
This is the brutal truth of a system that
punishes with fear, the white boy cloaked in
anonymity, spreading hate under the
watchful leer.
But the black boy stands resilient, a true
warrior against the false front, fighting
through struggles, while acknowledging
what society often daunts.
Among faces of all colors, race becomes a wedge
driven deep, while the black boy rises with
dignity that systemic injustice won't keep.
Racism is learned, it's not innate; an echo of
fear and disdain, while figures like
Congressman King spin division, ignoring
history's strain.
I share the vision of Martin King—a dream
where all men stand tall, where black men
are cherished, seen, respected, as equals to
us all.

Blossom

Here I am, a forgotten child, a seed buried in the dirt, counted out and given up on by the world a resilient seed that has sprouted from beneath concrete into a rose that no one expected to bloom. (Roué) A man devoted to a life of sensual pleasure sensual as in intelligence and awareness. My mind is prickly, often ascending into flourishing shrubs with divided leaves, and brightly colored are my thoughts, a fragrant breeze that clears the senses.

I am the face of every Black child in the ghetto, the embodiment of those Black men and women gunned down or unjustly incarcerated. Militant, I stand tall for you—blossomed, strong, humble, and hardened. Rest in peace, Trayvon Martin

Boredom

Racing against time, I often find myself alone,
ready to drive until the tires wear down to the
bone.
Running barefoot like a Flintstone, unyielding
in my quest, I push on, refusing to halt,
ignoring all the rest, even after my shoes
dissolve into debris, no comfort beneath my
feet, still, I forge ahead, struggling to find
my own heartbeat.
Like Jesus bearing his cross under the oppressive
sun, I carry my burdens; the weight is never
done.
Where am I headed? Only time will reveal,
But every step I take, I fight through the pain I
feel.
With sweat rolling down, and doubt whis-
pering near, I embrace the struggle,
pushing past the fear.
This journey is relentless, yet I refuse to quit,

for within this chaos lies my strength, my
spirit lit.
No matter how far or how long this road may
swell,
I'll keep racing against time, only time will tell.

Breakin' News

The mind is the sharpest and most formidable weapon in the battle for strength, the pursuit of wealth where shadows stretch long, crossing the breadth, dreams take flight on wings of ambition, soaring high in the landscape of thoughts, let your hopes never die. With each sunrise, a canvas fresh and bright, painted with purpose, each stroke ignites the light fortune favors the brave, those hearts that dare to carve paths in the silence, the burdens we bear. Steel your resolve, let courage ignite in the depths of despair, find a flicker, a light, dreams are the treasures hidden deep within the soul, unveil them with wisdom, let your spirit be whole.

The battle is fierce, the road is often steep, but the mind's powerful grip on faith strengthens deep. We navigate storms with vision as we sail in the ocean of challenges, we rise and we prevail.

Wealth's in your heart not just in your hand, the riches of kindness spread through the land, gather those dreams, let them blossom and bloom, in the garden of life let hope fill the room.

Each thoughts a soldier, each ideas a shield, together they go hand and hand refusing to yield. In the arena of doubt where shadows often creep, the mind's fortitude climbs mountains so steep. So walk with conviction, let the passion be your guide in the quest for fulfillment. Fear will subside, for as you conquer the battles within your own sphere, remember with an open mind the path is made clear. Fortune favors the brave, the dreamers who strive, the mind is a sword, a spirit that's alive, for the mind is the weapon, the key to the fight. In the journey of life, let your spirit take flight.

Caged by Circumstance:

A JOURNEY THROUGH DARKNESS AND SURVIVAL

I remember back in '94, my mom was smokin' dope. Imagine your own mother lockin' you in a closet just to get high, fillin' her lungs with crack smoke. My brothers and I grew up heartless and hopeless—it's just how it is comin' up in poverty, used to seein' black lives lost to overdose. No drug addiction for me, but my grandma was definitely an alcoholic; she was a different person with a shot glass and some music playin'.

Ready, set, here we go. I was only 12 when I first encountered weed smoke, catchin' a contact high at such a young age. By the time I was four, I had no guidance, faith, or hope. I wasn't wishin' for a father, he was a joke, Johnny Knoxville-Steve-O. I never knew him, so I vowed never to attend his funeral. My youth was troubled, my mind burdened, it could leave you comatose just thinkin' about it. I've seen darkness and gone places you wouldn't dare or want to go. While she was gettin' high, a toddler I was crawlin' out of a window from the second floor.

My mother wasn't a queen, more of a hustler, and our

house wasn't a home. With so many men coming and goin' , you'd think it was a grocery store. Trustin' women is hard, she fed me that reality from my high chair.

And I won't stop there. At 14, hearin' that my girlfriend water broke, I was still livin' with my mom, who relied on the government. I had no job, I was broke. I was just a kid. People shook their heads and told me a man handles his business. A man who doesn't care for his child doesn't allow that child to grow. The streets and time taught me this. With a young mind, all I could think about was survival, especially since I had a kid of my own now. I had to find a way to provide. The Bible says Jesus turned water into wine, well, this pistol in your face will turn your dollars into mine. It was late and cold, maybe winter. My conscience abandoned me, and I came off harsh with the butt of a gun. Three and a half years was my sentence, the max was a dime. Here I am, a convicted felon at 16, doin' state time.

Childhood's Illusions

When you're just a kid, life feels as pure and serene as a dove nesting on pillows of open clouds. In childhood, worries seem non-existent, your only concern is what's going to fill your belly, keeping hunger at bay before you rest your head, eager for tomorrow's adventures. You're cheerful, waking up with a smile. At least, that's true for some of us.

But where I grew up, sunny days were scarce. Hopelessness, sadness, and depression lingered like perpetual dark clouds. You learn the difference between right and wrong as though these words alone could guide you through life, offering a clear path forward. Yet, in the darkness, right and wrong become mere words, lacking action, you become blind, an additional part of the human centipede commonly known as "the blind leading the blind."

As a kid, you don't ponder the future. Sure, you might hear people talk about it, but where I come from, dreaming felt hard. We were taught self-hate, taught to kill and become our own worst enemies under the gaze of our oppressors. As children, the adult world's shadows and racism didn't cloud our minds yet.

At 14, life blindsided me with unforeseen responsibility. Holding my own child in my arms, the weight of innocence and vulnerability mirrored in his eyes consumed me. I was just a child myself, unprepared for the journey of parenthood amidst a world already heavy with its burdens.

By 16, I found myself trapped in a cell, day in and day out, facing the cold isolation of solitary confinement. The corrections officer's lie was what sat me down for those harrowing 365 days in administrative segregation. I was stripped of my youth and freedom, replaced by an endless monotony that gnawed at my spirit.

And yet, they call it "corrections." Why label it so when self-help books like "The Best Resource Directory For Prisoners" and "How To Start Your Own Business When You Get Out Of Prison" remain on the restricted list?

They ignore the emergency light. I witnessed a man having a seizure during a fistfight in his cell, he could have lost his life. Witnessing such things only hardens you. Imagine being thrown to the ground while being assaulted, hearing nothing but "stop resisting," while your arms are already pinned behind you in handcuffs.

Each experience etched harsh lessons on my young soul, challenging the fragile boundaries between innocence and survival.

John Thomas

Crafting Success from Setbacks

Why accept failure when success is free?
No such thing as failure exists while oxygen still reaches the brain and allows your lungs to breathe.
The world is yours, you just have to open your mind and allow your eyes to see.
Turn dreams into reality, the summit's not steep.
Strength in adversity, let resilience reign,
Life's a canvas, you're the artist, paint with no refrain.
Manifest greatness, let doubt be slain.
Opportunities endless, fortune in the lane.
Success is the journey, not just the end.
Rise from the ashes, let your spirit transcend.
Let passion be the compass, let wisdom lead,
Sow seeds of perseverance, harvest the creed.
In the face of failure, don't retreat or cower,
For every setback holds the seed of power.

Stand tall in the storm, let your vision be clear,
Harness the strength within, conquer every fear.
Each breaths a chance, each days a new page,
Craft your legacy, shine on life's stage..

Cutting Loose Ends

I compromised who I was to appease others all the while I was dyin inside battling myself drowning, slipping into a deep depression. Everybody I knew had their hand out for something except to pull me from the solitary darkness when I was losing me, sleeping at minimum because all I've had was broken dreams.

Everybody's prepared for the take off to soar high on cloud 9 above land and streams but nobody wants to fall. You can't learn to fly when you're living with a broken wing.

One minute l felt close to you, other times I didn't roller coasters take you up and down, side to side, round and round. Our love was a roller coaster, nothing but entertainment in your amusement park. Vehemently elated I wanted to shine in the light so badly that I got left in the dark. It might be always sunny in Philadelphia but this ain't Philadelphia my heart is disfigured on the inside. Every memoir is mar. Psalm 91:13 tells you the devil was a serpent. I tried to pull you out the mud but here you are trying to drown me on purpose. And to think l was over that feeling you get when you lose a person, that feeling have yo' stomach in knots. I've shed more tears than water has run down a shower curtain. I stand as a man mentally battered l was hurtin', never thought I'd see the day a bitch would make me cry, did you love me or hate me seems like you can't decide. I was supposed to change into a Superman like Clark Kent. I tried that but I'm still stuck here in the lowest lane mundanely estranged. My heart becomes as cold as winter when it rains. That same heart used to beat for you. So high off you l used to be somewhere amongst the stars when you'd visit my mind now when l think of you I don't see anything as if I was born blind but I still want the best for you, being spiteful or bitter that ain't how I'm designed. Cuttin' ties.

12/11/23 - 12/22/23

Dear America

Dear America,

I never chose for my skin to be black, nor did I ask for my ancestors to endure the horrific violence of molestation and rape, which tainted their DNA and ultimately gifted me a lighter pigment. Yet despite this blend, I've encountered 50 shades of hate. Somewhere along this tangled lineage lies a trace of Caucasian blood, weaving itself into the very fibers of my being, reminding me that, in essence, every man is declared equal—as the Bible professes. I am not the architect of this world; it was thrust upon me. I wasn't given the luxury to select the circumstances of my creation. No, I was assigned this black identity in a world marred by corruption and dripping with envy and hatred.

I am a kaleidoscope of colors, an individual who seeks depth within rather than being confined to the simple labels of race. But hold on—let me clarify; don't misconstrue my words. Out of 206 nationalities that blanket this earth, who decided that white people should be the benchmark of superiority? I have questions that demand answers, and I long for you to look me in the eye as we spar with these truths. Yet, more often than not, I find you turning your back, hastily retreating on your heels. And yet, this is America, where I am both bewildered and outraged by the fact that, until February 7, 2013, Mississippi reiterated through the 13th Amendment that Black people could still be viewed and treated as property.

This land, branded as the home of the brave and the land of the free, often denies the same freedoms to black men like myself. I urge you to awaken your consciousness; what you perceive may not be the whole truth. These are stark realities—so-called truths masquerading as lies. Delve deep within, for there lies the real essence of truth. In this moment, the Bible, fear, self-doubt, and a government that cultivates confusion have you under a spell. It's disheartening to acknowledge that while they celebrate your achievements, they secretly wish to witness your downfall.

Deprogrammed

It hurts being a slave but it's when you willin' to stay one, chains on your mind, complacency weighs a ton. Freedom's a dream that we grasp with our fists in a world where oppression and poverty persist. We fight for our rights, for a taste of the air,
where equality lives and justice is fair.
Generations before us bled for our chance to break from the cycle, to rise up and advance.
Their spirits are with us, their struggles our guide,
in the face of adversity, with strength we abide.
But some stay in comfort, in chains they've accepted, blind to the power that's been long neglected. They tell us we're free, yet the prisons overflow, with the majority of blacks whose progress is slow. So why is it called Corrections?

The system is broken, it's designed to confine,
our potential is stifled, our futures undermined.
The media blinds us with visions so fake,
distractin' our minds, our spirits they seek to break. Economic oppressions the new form of chains, keepin' us in poverty, bound by financial pains. But knowledge is power, break free from the chains, elevate and make change, educate the mind and with due time, truth will shine bright and radiant.
Knowledge is key, unlockin' the chains of my mind,
Wisdom is enveloped in a shadow realm where the truth's hard to find.
Self-awareness breaks the shackles, minds unchained from the reins, deprogrammings just the start to cleanse our minds of the stains that were once etched in our brains.
Knowledge is wisdom. Wisdom is purpose, forging paths through hardships, turmoil and pain.

Don't risk happy for happier

If you try to control what's out of your control,
it controls you, tough times don't last,
tough people do. But what about the days
when the sun doesn't shine?
When the world's on your shoulders and you
feel like you on a tightrope toein' the line?
In them moments, dig deep and remember your
core, the storms make you stronger, they
hard to ignore. Every scar is a story, each
wound tells a tale,
of battles you've conquered, and times you
prevailed. Look in the mirror, see the
fighter inside,
with every struggle, you've learned to confide.
In the darkest of nights, when the light's hard to
find, your spirit's a beacon, your heart
redefined.
Life's not a straight path, it twists and it bends,

but with courage and love, the journey
transcends.
Embrace the chaos, the uncertainty too,
for it's moldin' the person who's undeniably
you.
Don't seek perfection, it's a flawed pursuit,
find joy in the journey, your passions recruit.
In the face of defeat, rise up and renew,
with every setback, a chance to breakthrough.
The beauty in life's in the lessons we learn,
through pain and through joy, the fires we
burn.
It's not about control, but the grace to let go,
to trust in the process and the seeds that
you sow.
So hold onto hope when the skies turn grey,
remember your strength in the face of dismay.
Tough times shape you, they forge something
new,
And at the end of the storm, there's a clearer
view.
With heart and with grit, you'll find your way
through, for tough times don't last, but
tough people do..

Embracing Madness as a Path to True Freedom

A deceleration of insanity is a form of censorship and control/
Tryin' to tame the chaos within, to fit the societal mold/
But the mind's a wild beast, it's hard to hold, it resists the chains/
Silencin' the voices only amplifies the pain/
Creativity smothered under layers of restraint/
Where the vibrant hues of thought are forced to be faint/
Expression stifled by the fear of dissent/
Imagination suffocated, dreams met their end/
But in the cracks of conformity, rebellion will sprout/
A spark in the darkness, a whispered shout/
For true freedom lies in embracin' the whole/
Not just the fragments that fit in a predetermined role/
So let the mind run free, let it roar and unfold/

For in the depths of madness, there's a beauty untold/
In the symphony of chaos, the soul finds its voice/
Breakin' free from the shackles, makin' its own choice..

Enigmatic Da Vinci Within

Sometimes my mind drifts, taking me on journeys I can hardly comprehend; perhaps it's the Huey Newton within me. With pen to paper, my mind's eye paints vivid pictures, unsure where to share them. Signals traverse from my brain to my wrist, urging my right hand to embrace the challenge. A troubled man like Marvin Gaye, I find solace in autopilot, letting my spirit wander free as I ride these lines harmoniously. I fear no man, only my limitations can bring me down. Within my mind, I hold treasures like the ocean floor; knowledge uplifts me, and the journey to success is endless. In my late twenties, quiet yet imposing, my words can overwhelm, much like Jay Reed in "In Too Deep." I don't chase dreams, I live another life when I sleep. In my world, dreams often lead to rap stars and athletes, or to those imitating Ace Boogie's lifestyle. But I strive for greater heights, balanced between self-preservation and humility, though when provoked, I can shift toward the darker side. Swift as a panther, even in daylight, I forewarn: trying to decipher me is like suicide. I am the enigmatic Morse code, a young, modern Da Vinci.

Entering The System

I gaze through an empty window at a distant gray sky, gun towers are watchin', their shadows drawn at night. Double razor fences cut sharp through the day, what do they call this place—prison? A world gone astray.
Solitary confinement, chaos thrives in the hall,
life outside continues on but I'm sitting frozen, appalled.
Time here is stagnant like sun's pull on earth,
a black truck rolls daily, markin' my worth.
The calendar shifts slowly, seasons flicker and fade,
heat breaks in summer, winter's chill invades.
Endless hours stretch onward, mental battles I fight,
awake or asleep, the torment feels tight.
Years without hope, just dreamin' to rest.

With eyelids closed tight, I escaped from this test.
But reality kicks in, just a blink, and I'm there,
awake in confinement, trapped deep in my stare.
Loneliness gnaws at me, fear swells in my chest,
savage rage bubblin', no solace, no rest.
Scars etched on my soul, no words can define as life flows around me, like a hand turnin' wine.
Prison, a hellish phase, an experiment of time,
a subject for study, caught in my prime.
Thought I was invincible, too tough to be bent,
yet the system's tight grip proved a cruel descent.
I bore all the weight, acceptin' each lash,
trapped in this body, but my spirit won't crash.
Each struggle endured, my pride began to swell,
In this dark, bitter place, I covered my shell.
Prison was a picture, a scene on the screen,
Locked-Up Raw and Oz—the life I had seen.
4/28/99, just a ward of the state, pops turned away, mom lost in her fate.
The streets taught my lessons, resilience as my creed, to provide for a child, I'd do what I need.
Go for broke or C.R.E.A.M, cash flows in streams,
but the choices I made led to shattered dreams.
Tried as an adult, just sixteen and raw,

shipped upstate, swallowed whole by the law.
Jay said, should've got involved with rhythm
instead I got lost in the system.

Fighting for Inner Peace

My inner me is my enemy, I'm my only competition, fightin' shadows in my mind, it's a constant occupation, lost in self-reflection, a maze of contemplation, wrestlin' with my demons seekin' salvation.

Eyes in the mirror don't lie, they see the pain. In the storm of my thoughts, tryin to evade the rain, self-doubt creeps in, it's a silent invasion, confidence shatters under heavy persuasion.

Voices in my head often whisper, when ignored they shout, dark thoughts creep in tryin' to drown me out in attempt to control my mind and fill my heart with doubt, every step I take feels like a calculation, strugglin' to break free from this mental incarceration..

Fly With Me

Take hold of my hand, come fly with me far away from the sadness of betrayal, loneliness, and fear, away from the pain, hurt, abandonment, learned prejudices, and poverty. Fly with me to a place of happiness, smiles, plenty of laughter, and fond memories; a place of peace, love, and joy, surrounded by tall trees, delicate animals, waterfalls, and nothing but every imaginable fruit to eat.

Fly with me to a place where the oxygen has no corrosion, where the grass is forever green, where the sun always shines, and the sky is always blue. Even at nighttime, there's always a full moon, accompanied by a universe of stars with a sight that's astonishingly beautiful.

Fly with me to a place where love conquers all

things, where when the wind blows, there's a sensation of passion as the breeze caresses your skin, a place you don't have to close your eyes to escape to feel free. Take my hand and let's go to that place in harmony.

Fragility of Blood:

TRUST AND BETRAYAL WITHIN FAMILY BONDS

You have to consider yo family sometimes in the same light as you'd view a stranger.
You can see through water, you can't see through blood.
Family will show signs of respect but will stab you in the back without a reason sometimes it's just because.
Jealousy and envy be the seeds that they sow actin' like they love you but you never really know.
Shared DNA, but the loyalty's weak, like a neglected dog they could stray any day.
It's a cold realization when the trust starts to crack,
the ones you hold closest could be plottin' an attack.
Blood ties ain't a promise, it's a fragile facade,
they might smile in your face while they're stealin' your nod.

You can either learn a lesson or be a lesson and
learn the hard way, truth ain't always
kind, sometimes the ones you cherish and
hold close are the ones who undermine.
Family might be blood, but they ain't always
the ones that reciprocate the love.
Sometimes even blood can turn deceptive like
an option have to keep yo love selective.
Water is clear, blood can be thick and if a well
can run dry family can break quick..

From Fear to Acceptance

The things I saw in you were unmatched, unique, and unfamiliar, which filled me with fear. In my uncertainty, I ran—from life, from love, from everything. Inexperienced, I didn't know how to handle it. I had once given my all to one woman—many called it puppy love—but when you grow up without acceptance, it's easy to crave someone's affection. I didn't anticipate being left vulnerable, hurt, and scarred, which darkened my heart.

Initially, with you, it was purely physical—lust. But that quickly transformed into something deeper—us, as in love. It was a love I wasn't prepared for. How could I love you when resentment still resided within me? All you offered was love, hoping that one day the pain within me would dissipate, allowing a new beginning and freedom to breathe life into our future.

I tried to do right by you, but no man is perfect. The struggles I put you through were unjust. How could I ask you to reconsider us after causing such hurt? Yet, I'm willing to try because I've experienced the grass on the other side and realized nothing compares to what I see in your eyes.

How does one choose which path to take when both feet are planted? Do you continue a path that pleases others but tears you apart inside, or do you follow what feels right, listening to your heart? My heart belongs to you, though you might doubt it, wondering how love can persist after all you've endured.

My answer lies in our shared nature; we became flawed the moment Eve gave Adam the fruit. Watching the movie Fences, I saw you in its narrative. You gave selflessly, offering what you believed was your all and were ready to face any obstacle beside me, as love often demands. I didn't realize then, but as I reflect, no woman alive evokes what I feel for you. You have no comparison.

From Heartbreak to Self-Discovery

Burnt a few bridges in the process built
my own,
through some of the worst times of my life I've
had to stand alone. Carved my own path
through turmoil and pain, found my own
truths even when I couldn't see past the
pouring rain.
I've had to struggle in silence with pain unseen,
fought through the mud and emerged clean.
Mistakes in my past were lessons in disguise.
They taught me who's fake and who's wearin' a
disguise. Those are the ones afraid to look
you in the eyes for fear you'll see their lies.
Broke a few hearts, including my own. They say
history repeats itself so how to love is an
emotional trait I learned on my own. My
mother was busy tryin to find her identity
and my pops, well he left one day and never
returned home. So imagine the hurdles I

took to pick up the pieces and kept movin'
alone.
Honesty's a curse, but I wear it well,
Iived through the struggle with stories to tell.
I've fallen a thousand times, but pulled myself
back up from the pits of hell with every
ambition to pravile.
Shattered dreams forged my soul from the cold,
the mistakes from my past made me whole,
no regrets, every stumble, through the
depths of my struggles, I discovered my
soul.

From Me to YOUth

Put the guns down, there's other ways to generate revenue. You were born with the tools you just have to believe in yourself. Take it from me there's nothing cool about endin' up in a cell or being carried by six. Life's about more than beefin' on the net, rappin' about ops, disrespectin' the dead, and carryin' sticks.

I was once in your shoes, went to prison at 16, made APB, never thought I'd make the news. I've had ops too, stomped a brother out, put him in a coma. And for what because we were with different crews.

I ain't preachin' to you, nah, just givin' you the game about what certain paths can lead to. Ten years is a decade you go away for that long how many people you think gone have you.

The streets aren't loyal, they'll turn on you in a heartbeat. I've seen too many dreams die in the night, across the hall from my cell I can tell you what it's like to witness a man put a sheet around his own neck and try to put an end to his life. Once diagnosed with PTSD you'll never be fully alright.

Young'n you think you invincible, that bullets don't hurt, but every shot fired just adds to the dirt. It's a cycle of violence, a never endin' game, but in the end, all you are left with is shame either that or a grave. 458917 is what they called me in them prisons. Being addressed as a number so much can make you forget you were even born with a name.

I look at you and see the potential, don't throw it away. Life's too precious to waste in a cage. The world is bigger than the block or your hood. You could rise above if you just understood.

Education is the key, knowledge is power. Build a future, hour by hour. Invest in yourself, believe in your worth. Your mind is a weapon, more deadly than any generational curse.

Success isn't measured by the chain on your neck or the fear in your eyes when holdin' a gun. It's the legacy you leave, the lives that you touch, the love that you give, not the hate you clutch.

Respect isn't earned just because you can squeeze the trigger of a gun. It's about the man you are, the battles you've won. The battle to stay true, to rise above strife, to value each moment in life. A future cut short by a senseless act has no comin' back from a bullet's impact. Think about your family, the ones you love, and the pain in their eyes when push comes to shove because ain't no comin' back once that green line goes flat. If you could start your life from scratch you couldn't change that.

Life's about choices, put down the guns, let go of the hate. Choose life, before it's too late.

Dream big, aim high, don't settle for less. You're worth more than a grave or a bulletproof vest.

Look up to the leaders, all old heads ain't haters plenty of em have stories it's just on you to open your mind and listen before you open your mouth. I can give you the game about what I've been through with hopes you don't take that route and I'm still at the bottom but I won't allow the likes of my oppressor to influence me to pull another black man down to make it out. They taught us to use our fist, not our brains for clout. But take it from a man who got through the lows by seein' the highs.

Success is a journey, seen through an open mind.

Grit, Growth, and Resilience

You have two lives, the second one begins when you realize you only have one. I'm from the projects a place that's dark even when the forecast tells you in the sky you'll see the sun, the project taught me the grind I'm from where dreams get crushed survival of the fit' in this game, ain't no rush.

Life's a chessboard, pawns fall first, protect your queen schemin' on the come-up, every move, every scene, from nickel and dime to daydreamin' about million-dollar schemes chasin' paper, but the streets still haunt my dreams. Life's a hustle, every day a new test, enemies in disguise, gotta watch who I impress. From corner to corner, dodgin' the feds and the law.

Money, power, respect, still I wanted more, its in my blood, the struggle made me who I am from the guttah to the throne, I'm the man with a plan. Legends are made, through the fire and the pain grit and grind, every loss, every gain, haters wanna see you fall, but I rise above

stacking blueprints, turnin' hate into love this life's a

gift, and I'm tryin' to live it large Bentleys and yachts, but it's somethin about the streets they still leave scars. Friends turned foes, loyalty's a ghost trust few, keep my circle close. Diamonds on my neck, but the weight's heavy still, money can't buy peace, it's a different kind of thrill.

Every day I awake the overall goal is to make it out of the mud, but the dirt's still on my shoes. They say success is bittersweet, I said sometimes you win to lose. Legacy on my mind, buildin' empires from scratch from the block to the boardroom, making every match, so here's to the hustle, the grind never stops livin' life to the fullest, until my heartbeat drops.

From the shadows to the spotlight, I don't want to conquer the game you can have it all I want is the money and to die a martyr show that's the

living proof, you can rise, no matter the shame..

Hate Is An Inverted Love

Hate is but an echo of love turnt on its head, a fiery tempest where gentle whispers once tread.
Passion's twin wrapped in anger's fierce grasp,
a mirror reflectin' love, yet with a darker rasp.
Where warmth once lingered, now cold winds rise transformin' soft caresses into harsh, bitter sighs.
Love's light, when fractured, casts shadows so long,
Turnin' sweet serenades into hauntin' , bitter songs.
Inverted love flows like a river that runs deep,
Where we once sowed joy, now resentment we reap. It twists affection into jagged lines,
transformin' cherished moments into sharp confines. What was once cherished now bears the sting of blame, where devotion flourished, now resides only shame. Love's

garden, once fertile, now choked by dark weeds, where hate grows feral, love's once-nurtured seeds. Yet within hate's fierce and unyieldin' core, lies the remnants of love we cannot ignore. Emotions born from bonds once strong, twisted by the hurt when things go wrong.

Intense as passion, hate fuels the night, both birthed from need, neither wrong nor right. Two sides of a heart's relentless beat, in their complexity, love and hate meet. In this dark mirror, we clearly see how closely intertwined both emotions can be.

For hatred, searing bright, is love inverted,

Wrapped in the darkness, passion is thwarted.

It whispers truths we're afraid to hear, about the depth of loss and the power of fear. In hate's harsh glare, clarity emerges, the shadow love casts when disparity surges. Yet through the storm of emotions this strong, the line between the two isn't clear or long. For in hate's fierce burn, there's a spark of what was true, the remnants of love's flame, still burnin' through. To understand hate, is to grasp love's plight, two forces entwined in eternal fight.

A testament to the power both feelings share, in love's absence, hate draws near. But in redemption lies a tangled embrace with a chance to transform and revive love's grace. For in recognizin' the source of hate's fire, we can reignite love's desire.

Hi ladies

Ashanti, Free, Eve, Cassie, Nicki Minaj, Love & Hip-Hop's Emily, Sydney Carter, Vita & Mel B – no scratches or hickeys, I just want to take you down. Not to mention I'm a freak, so first I want to nose dive, letting my tongue dig deep in your ocean sea. Alicia Keys I won't tell your secret, so after we do the unthinkable, Swizz Beatz will never hear about it from me. – Beyoncé I'm dangerously in love with your goddess physique, and all I need is one night if you let me undress and caress your hourglass antique; bet I'll be that one secret you keep from Jay-Z.

Never have I been addicted to prescriptions; a hood dude, besides that dirty money, bringing women to a climax has always been my philosophy (medicine). – Keyshia Cole, Nia Long, Eva Mendes, Paula Abdul, and Tatyana Ali don't you be on that foolery. Like R. Kelly said, your every fantasy I will fulfill as long as you sex me. I'm a woman's kryptonite; an orgasm is guaranteed satisfactory, but I'm a dog, so as you can see, I'm only about making toes curl. You holler out in tongue as I leave you weak in the knees, and I got a humongous appetite; I love women outside of Mya, Faith Evans, movie exec. Tracey Edmonds, Lil' Kim, and Halle Berry. I'll stroke and probe Katy Perry and let Jessica Alba and Megan Fox come set on my face; my tongue will transform that sweetness into a waterfall. Your potion is like honey, and your juices I'm just itching to taste, I'm yearning to taste Lucy Liu, sexy single Kara Hawkins, Melanie Fiona, Olivia, and Nicole Scherzinger — well, really the entire Pussycat Doll group.

My sex drive is astronomical (extremely large), and my craving for the female body is beyond the earth's atmosphere like astronomy breaststroke. I want to swim inside Meagan Good missionary until I'm waist deep, waist deep in that sweetness. We can sixty-nine; I eat you while you suck me, or I can beat it up, beat it up until that ass dozes off to sleep. Letoya Luckett cried she was torn on the single of her break release, well I can piece it back together; don't believe, come see 'bout me a love doctor, I can be that sexual healing. A dose of this antidote of me is what you need; let me bend it over, pull your hair while you throw it back to the rhythms of Al Green.

I can only imagine what it's like having sex with Rihanna all alone, and she screams out in the open birthday suit under cascades of infamous rain. Your nails dig into the flesh of my chest while drops of rain dance on your face as you tilt your head up to the sky and embark on this furious roller coaster ride, or we can reenact something out of the pages of Zane, Sex Chronicles since you get excited by the thought of whips and chains. I'll handcuff your hands to the headboard and eat that sweetness till it hurricanes and won't refrain even if you let the neighbors know my name, but until I see the tears in your eyes, a prediction of rain.

And nah, I don't want to be with every girl in the world, just a selective few like those females I already mentioned,Kyla Pratt, Sanaa Lathan, and Zoe Saldana, Skylar Diggins, Raven Symone, video vixen Emmaly Lugo, and Amber Rose. I want to lick you up and down and groove between your legs until I become in tune with your mind, body, and soul, and every memory thereafter will make you squeeze your legs tight together, suffocating one of your pillows. Aquarius is my zodiac description; I'm a freak I must admit until the saga continues, I want Tyra Banks, Keri Hilson, La La, and Sade, Miley Cyrus, Jordan Sparks, Diamond of Crime Mob, Super Head, and Selena Gomez, sexy single Crystal Thomas from out in D.C.—hi ladies...

December, 24, 2011

Hidden behind a smile

You ever see a angel die in rare form when the halo falls, you feel the devil's storm and it feels like I've been burnin' wings since the day I was born. I might look like I'm good, but I'm hurtin' inside,
sometimes I cry, you don't see the tears. I've become an expert at harborin' what I feel inside.
The smile on my face is just a mask,
behind these eyes, there's a pain that won't pass. Maybe it stems from my moms, maybe the absence of my dad or grand-mother, how I was treated from the trauma in the past. Maybe it's just being black havin' to live with the fact that every breath I take could potentially be my last, in white America where the value of my life holds no merit when in comparison to a police officer's badge. Martin Lee Anderson

was beat in boot camp 'til he died in a ambulance, that boy was 15 years old forget what they say he did. Tell me how I'm supposed to feel when police killin' kids?

They say life's a gift, but it feels like a curse,
trapped in my mind, and it keeps gettin' worse.
I'm drownin' in thoughts, can't catch my breath,
fightin' with demons suicidal thoughts has me runnin' from death.
The nights are the hardest, when I'm all alone,
battlin' shadows, scared to close my eyes, that's when they hunt my dreams like Robert Englund when he wore the glove and had that red and black sweater on. I'm screamin' for help, but it echoes in vain, lost within a storm inside myself that won't wash away the pain.
Every day's a war, but I'm losin' the fight,
wagin' battles in the dark all the while runnin' from the light. I might look like good, but I'm breakin' apart, walkin' through life with a shattered heart.
I put on this facade, pretendin' I'm strong but I'm scarred and flawed.
They don't see the nights where I'm restless, ready to throw in the towel and my soul levitate like a balloon. People don't check on you, they just think you immune 'cause you don't cry when in pain, you just keep lickin' the wound.

I'm stuck in a loop of chasin' peace that always
appears far out of sight, but I keep it inside
lettin' the world believe that I'm okay,
while I silently grieve lost in this ride,
caught in a battle between truth and pride.
Sometimes I cry, but the tears never show,
locked in a struggle within myself that
nobody knows.

If I was white for a day

If I woke up white, skin bright like the moonlight,
walkin' through the day without a hint of fright.
No stares, no glares, from folks unaware of the struggles I face or the burdens I bear.
Doors open wide, opportunities on my side,
no need to justify, just take the ride.
Police pass me by, no suspicion in their eye,
livin' life on easy mode not a fear to pry.
I'd use the day to understand the privilege at hand, and vow to fight harder when I convert back into a black man.
If I woke up white, skin bright like the moonlight,
walkin' through the day without a hint of fright.
I'd see the blind spots, the gaps in the tale,
where justice is partial, and systems still fail.

Privilege ain't earned, it's a birthright bestowed,
a deck that's stacked in the lives that we mold.
My skin would be armor, a shield from the blows that people of color face in highs and in lows.
I'd walk in their shoes, but with invisible ease,
a stranger to their struggles, immune to their pleas.
I'd question the silence, the comfort in lies, the ignorance that's blinding so many eyes.
Back in my skin, I'd fight twice as hard to break down the barriers to dismantle the guard.
Understanding the depth, the layers unseen
of inequality's curse of a world so mean.
If I was white, they'd see my worth without a fight,
but in this skin I shine, my spirit's bright,
resilience in my roots, standin' tall through every plight..

If Life Was Real Would You Fake It

What if life were a dream, revealing to you, in the depths of your slumber, every misfortune you could have prevented or every warning you could have given another about the inevitability of fate, like death? What if you possessed the awareness unlike the other being of the exact moment another person would come into existence? Would you cherish every moment with that individual, pouring your heart into a shared experience? Or would you bluntly impart the weight of the knowledge you carried, aware of what lay ahead for them? Perhaps you'd choose to observe that soul from a distance, feeling a blend of pity and sorrow.

Now, consider yourself: what if you were keenly aware of the day when sleep became not a fleeting reprieve but an eternal certainty? How would you react? Even if you somehow managed to save your life, what would become of your soul amidst such a reality?

Imagine if that dream laid bare every decision you were destined to make, illuminating the daring consequences or unveiling each avoidable circumstance you faced. How would you navigate your life once you awoke and grappled with the truth of your existence?

If you've lived your life differently, in ways that stray from your current path, then what was the reason behind sleeping on life in the first place? Change is simple, yet perhaps the simplest thing to do is to learn. Learn as you journey through the experiences life offers, using them as tools and a foundation for your growth.

In the Shadows of Love: A Struggle Between
Light and Dark
Depression lives in a body that fights to
survive,
while my weary mind whispers, "You'd be
better off deprived."
Somewhere in the shadows, it dawned on me
that nightmares don't dissolve just because
the eyes see.
I seek the answers, askin' , "Why am I still
here?
A harsh reality, not just shadows of fear.
Caught in a tug-of-war 'tween heaven and
hell,
where love turns to hate, and it's hard to excel.
I want to be loved, but is it too late?
Hate echoed the final words that sealed our
fate.
Lately, I feel like Joe Goldberg in a twisted
play,
to love you truly, I must push you away.
So I've penned a letter, signed and sealed
tight,

hopin' you'll grasp it, find clarity in the fight.
I'm a monster by chance, never meant to be
cruel,
but you, you're pure love, a shimmerin' jewel.
I crave your affection, but fear the abyss, I don't
want to hurt you, what a perilous twist.
So here I stand, caught 'twixt dark and light,
wishin' for your love but longin' to take flight

In Your Gaze:

BUILDING TOMORROW FROM THE BEAUTY OF TODAY

When I look into your eyes, what lies is divine beauty in every description and despair. I see rare moments and temporary forevers , not too concerned with the past, and for that, I'd need a shovel, but I'm only trying to dig into your present, build a foundation, and call it the future.
But as I delve deeper, I'm lost in your essence, each heartbeat a compass, guiding my confessions,
In the silence, your whispers echo, a melody that soothes, breaking down my defenses,
Together we rise, unbound by the scars, painting our dreams beneath the shimmering stars.
In the shadows of doubt, your light shines through, a beacon of hope in a world so askew,

I've found a sanctuary in your embrace, where fears dissolve, and love takes its place,
Let's weave our destinies, stitch by stitch, in this tapestry of life, where we'll never switch.
With you, I've found a home, a place to belong, in the symphony of us, every note feels strong,
No need for tomorrow, let's live in today, with you by my side, I'm never astray,
For every moment spent in your gaze, is a chapter in a story that will never erase..

My heart outside my body you put the beat in my heart, and the air in my lungs. You made me smile when all else failed. At times when I want to throw it all away you gave me strength to put up a fight for one more day which has turned into 3 whole years. Looking back on the day you were born, in that hospital room you lay in my arms the most precious and prettiest thing I've ever seen up until now makes it almost impossible to hold back these tears watching you become the young woman you are throughout these years. Your first day of school you released my hand but left behind a face concealed with tears. I love you Jhenè and nothing will ever stop me from putting a smile upon your face. Daddy's girl you're not only my light and stars but you're my world, from your first laugh to your tiny hands in mine every moment with you feels so divine, watching you grow, every step you take.

No matter what I go through, you're the reason

my heart will never break. Through sleep-
less nights and joyful days in your eyes, I
see a thousand rays
of hope and love, you're a dream come true.
Jhenè, my angel, this love's for you
You've shown me life in a brand new light
with you everything's right, your giggles are
melodies, your hugs are pure in this crazy
world, my second coming you're my only
cure to a pain I wasn't so there was even a
cure.
So here's to you, my precious girl the one who
gave my life a whirl, daddy's here, through
thick and thin
With you, my love, let our journey have no end.

Journey Through the Eyes of a Troubled Mind

I'd be fooling myself if I claimed to be completely sane; at times, my mind is a battlefield, grappling with inner destruction like Kurt with the 40 in hand, Cobain!!. Depression has me feeling lost, like Caine when Mr. Johnson questioned if he cared about living or dying. Sometimes, when I shut my eyes, I wonder how it would feel if fate hit hard and I didn't come back after I was struck by that van. Catastrophes rage within; a Hurricane Katrina inside, and I find myself aching like Tyrese, ready to break down and let the tears flow. There's no need to question why; understanding requires a glimpse into the turmoil of my thoughts. It's a deeper excavation than a shovel can reach – more like J. Reid in 'In Too Deep'. The secrets I hide rival the beastly visage of that creature from Beauty and The Beast. If you're not liking what you see, move along, because all I can offer is my genuine self...

Just When I Thought I Found You

I know this might hit you out of the blue, but
from day one, I was drawn to you.
At first, it was your beauty, radiant and bright,
but as I learned your story, your soul
ignited my urge to see you in the light.
It was that void inside, the emptiness I sought
to fill, I'd leap into the abyss with you,
before I ever allowed you to die alone on
any hill.
You were a puzzle, complex and profound, and
I became obsessed, determined to piece you,
to be found.
In silence, I loved you, though those words
stayed locked tight, you seemed so torn, and
my truth might have felt like an
afterthought in your plight.
Not many men would leap when you called, but
when you did like a pilot I took flight, even

in darkness I saw the sun shining bright,
hidden in your eyes, a queen waiting to
ignite.
You ran, and I chased, a dance of push and pull.
Then out of nowhere you left, like a leaf in a
storm's cruel.
It bruised my pride, a wound hard to confess.
It's different to be turned away than to be asked
to assess.
I wanted you then, and somehow I still do,
I don't know what "forever" means, but I'd
choose no one but you.
Your beauty? Just a layer? your body I need not
dissect.
You've got the kind of essence that makes a
young man respect, But it's your driven
heart, your family-first mind, That truly
seals the deal, the strongest you I find.
You know what you want and sometimes push
too hard, you're fierce, independent, a
woman who's her own guard.
If you could read my thoughts, you'd see I'm an
open book, and the title of my story? It's
you, just take a look.
I ponder you often, what's on your mind
tonight?
How would your skin feel beneath my touch,
soft and light?
Do you ever think of "us," or the paths that we
could trace?
There's so much I long to say, but I won't string
you in this race.

So here's where I draw the line, with love and
peace, I'm gone, No puppeteer moves these
feelings, just a heart that's drawn.

Lack of Understanding

Lack of understandin' is where we fall short,
miscommunication got us all trapped,
blind to the truth, trapped in a maze,
conflicted stuck in our ways.
We talk but don't listen, words hit the wall,
echoes of silence, and we start to crawl
out the shadows, but the light blinds our eyes,
scared and afraid to see through the world's
disguise.
Fingers pointin', accusations fly high,
we're drownin' in this ocean of lies,
no empathy, just a cold hard stare.
We're lost in a world where no one cares.
Knowledge is power, but ignorance reigns
in the court of our minds, confusion remains,
we judge with our eyes, not with our souls.
If life was a motion picture we're all playin
unfair roles.
Hate breeds more hate, a cycle unbroken,

words like daggers, harshly spoken,
we can't see past our own reflections,
Deceit will always have you lost in a maze of misdirections.
Compassion fades in its place is greed,
humanity's lost in our selfish needs,
We climb over others in an attempt to reach the top,
not realizin' it's all gonna drop.
Truth's twisted, stories spun,
in the game of life, nobody's won,
we stumble, we fall, we lose our way,
in the end, we all pay..

Learning From Mistakes

I know it hasn't been easy being with me. I introduced you to a man who twisted your trust—selfish, inconsiderate, living every choice for myself instead of the "us" we should have been. Yet, somehow, you remained resilient, despite every reason to walk away. You were raised to fight, to hold on; I was not so fortunate. Without a father figure and watching my mother fall for men who couldn't see her worth, I grew blind to what a real woman embodies. I ran and ran while you stood steadfast, determined to offer me a love beyond the ordinary.

I had never known the embrace of genuine care, so love felt foreign, tightly fitting like an O.J. glove—too snug, uncomfortable, a reminder of my flaws. I became just another statistic, a man lost in the fog, unaware of my own identity. Now, I am left with a heavy heart filled with regrets, exposed, naked, and utterly alone. Alone in the haunting echo of your absence, I crave those moments when love bloomed like a balanced dance.

I stand here, ready to offer all of myself, hoping you'll

find the courage to reciprocate with your heart, mind, body, and soul. Allow me to wash away your tears; let me confront those walls of heartache with tender affection. Once we break through, I promise to delve deep within, bringing you not just joy and pleasure, but a sense of sanity that only true love can provide.

Learning to win through failure

In order to succeed, you must first learn to fail
every setback's a mere lesson it doesn't mean
you've taken an L. Failure's a teacher,
harsh but true, it's the grit in your soul, the
drive in you. Success comes with time and
with time company's many failures each
stumbles a step closer to the peak.
The language of loss doesn't exist, when you
can handle failure success starts to speak.
Embrace the fall, it's part of the climb in the
journey to greatness, it's just a matter of
time.

Life to a Glass of Water

A terrible thing to waste is the mind.

Unconsciously ignorant, I cradled my glass, cautious and careful, yet I failed to cherish it; it felt more like a lost opportunity than a blessing. My thoughts, stagnant and withered, left me mentally barren, as if I had neglected to cultivate the very soil of my existence. Given a shred of common sense, I would have covered my glass, yet what good would it have done? Every lid I attempted—a loose fit, a missed match, or a screw that just wouldn't hold —left me frustrated and perplexed. What eludes my understanding? I remain shrouded in confusion, while the precious water in my glass slowly evaporates, drop by agonizing drop.

On this winding journey of life, each spill echoes another year lost, irretrievable and fading away into the ether. Though my glass is not void, each misstep saps my strength, leaving me parched in body and spirit, a testament to my own ignorance. Stumbling through the darkness, I grapple with exhaustion and dehydration, all born from the folly of unawareness. Yet, every scrape and bruise teaches me; perhaps my stumbling was necessary for awakening. The realization that the reins of my destiny are mine to hold begins to take root.

As I gaze upon my glass, it shines with a quiet luminescence, whispering truths without uttering a word. In this moment of clarity, I understand that to halt the relentless evaporation, the simplest antidote is to drink the water that sustains me. But distracted by the chaotic ramblings of life, I am blind to the dryness of my throat, neglecting the nourishment I desperately seek.

Lost One's pt.2, Truth Is

Human beings, we are inherently gifted, each of us born with unique talents some of us with several. The right to be exceptional is not a lesson learned, nor is the path to intelligence a matter of choice. We come into this world brimming with intellectual potential, innate abilities that have been part of us since we first formed in the womb. Yet, for some, uncovering these treasures within our minds can be a struggle. We grapple with the challenge of accessing our full potential, of allowing our true purpose to blossom into reality.

One thing is certain: we are not here simply to exist and fade away. Our lives are meant to be a quest for meaning, a journey to seize life's purpose. Just as Martin Luther King Jr. left an indelible mark on history, or as The Beatles revolutionized music, our contributions echo throughout time. Even back to the age of the dinosaurs, the impact of our existence ripples through the ages, shaping the world and the lives intertwined with ours.

So, open your mind and look beyond the surface. Seek the clarity that eluded you upon first opening your eyes, and embrace the vast possibilities that await.

Lost Ones

Human beings, we as a collective, many of us find ourselves subjugated, enslaved within the confines of our own minds confused, feeble-minded, and bewildered about our true purpose in life.

In our desperation to escape the weight of existence, we abort our futures, including those of our children, searching for comfort in fleeting moments of relief. But once the pain subsides, we continue to live in a manner that is increasingly obscured and perplexing.

Cursed be the day of our birth! So many of us arrive in this world mired in confusion, molded and shaped into mere shadows of ourselves, zombies walking through life. We become hostages to materialism, gliding through existence as heartless victims rather than as intellectual or spiritual monuments.

Wandering aimlessly, we spend our lives chasing a misleading mirage, entranced by an illusion that feeds our inflated sense of self-worth. We opt for manipulation instead of manifesting our myriad thoughts into meaningful conclusions.

Detatched from the essence of reality, we seek a shallow definition of living, hoping to grasp harmony and bliss the ultimate state of happiness while remaining blissfully unaware of the truth. We forget that true fortune is attained through a genuine understanding of life. The health of your mind shapes the course of your life, determining the richness of your existence.

Love is Cursed by Monogamy

Love is cursed by monogamy. Consumed with abandonment and trust issues that constantly bothers me, fallin' in too deep unaware of the obvious, the bottom's steep. Often we swim in doubt where secrets creep, hidin' the pain within our mind skeleton's behind locked doors, but the echoes of the past still roar. Every "I love you" feels like a test, can't trust the words, love is cursed by monogamy. We often feel with our minds leavin' no room for the heart to contest.

To be on the path to forever is all that couples should know but most of us are caught up in the rapture where the primary focus is couple goals.

Caught in a loop of jealousy,
haunted by ghosts that we can't see,
fightin' for love, but the cost we settle for is
cheap.
Loyalty's a game, but who plays fair?
When nobody plays by the rules the expecta-

tions is lost when we don't care so loyalty
becomes but another word like despair.
Love's a battlefield, but we're losin' ground,
hearts buried in the trenches with no access or
trace to be found.
We at times find ourselves stuck in this twisted
bind chained to a love that's gone blind,
tryin' to fix what's already broken,
lost in the lies, but scared to leave, surrenderin'
to pride, suffocatin' in the emotions we try
to hide.
Promises like Metallica fade to black like smoke
in the night, and every touch just doesn't
feel right,
we hold on tight to what's left of us but trust is
gone, replaced by lust.
Caught in this cycle, some of us can't nor do we
care to break free, love is cursed by
monogamy. What is it that we can't see?
We fake a smile, play our parts,
but deep down, we're torn apart, livin' lies we
don't believe, trapped in what we're told or
deemed cool to be.
No happy endings in this story,
just broken dreams and faded glory.
Either remain subjugated or escape the love
cursed by monogamy that we helped
create...

Man's Search for Meaning

The two most important days in your life is the day you were born & when you find out why, the journey in between holds the truths that you must defy. From the cradle to the grave, we wrestle with our destiny in the shadows of our choices lies our true identity. Born into a world where the path is already paved yet the freedom to choose remains the greatest gift gave. Each heartbeat a question, each breath a silent vow to seek the reason in the now, not the when or the how.

Through trials and tribulations, the soul's tempered by fire, every failures a lesson, every setback a pyre

from the ashes of despair, we rise with new insight. The darkest nights of the soul give way to dawn's light. In the mirror of existence, our reflections often lie, we wear

masks to fit in, while our true selves cry but
in moments of stillness, when the world's at
bay we glimpse the divine, the purpose that
lights our way.
Purpose isn't found in gold, or the accolades
of men
it's in the silent moments, the whisper within
the din. It's in the love we give, and the
lives we touch. In the dreams we chase, and
the hearts we clutch.
To find why you were born, is to look beyond the
veil. To see the interconnected web, where
none of us can fail each thread is vital, each
life a crucial part in the grand tapestry,
woven by the heart.
The two most important days are but bookends
to a tale, a saga of discovery where even the
meek prevail. The journeys not the destina-
tion that defines our legacy in finding why
we truly learn what it means to be free.
For the answers lie within you, waiting to be
untied, the day you were born and the day
you find out why..

Me versus me

My outer world is pushin' me into a world that's shoving' me in a battle where it's me versus me.
When you lose money ultimately you lose nothin' but when you lose your character that's when you lose everythin'.
I'm caught in this maze, every turn feels the same,
chasin' after dreams, yet I'm losing in this game.
A clash of ambition, trapped in my own vision.
Every move scrutinized, every word dissected,
Strivin' for perfection, yet feelin' so neglected.
Faces all around me, but none that I trust, the mirror reflects a stranger in my eyes a facade of strength, hidin' silent cries.
These moments of clarity, few and far between in a world chasin' green, what does it all really mean?

I'm battlin' my demons, they're right under my skin, success on the outside, but the struggle's within. I look in the mirror, and I barely recognize the man starin' back, with the pain in his eyes.
They say money talks, but it can't buy peace, I'm learnin' the hard way, that pain don't cease.
Integrity's my armor, in this war I must win, each choice that I make defines who I am within.
I'm grindin' for more, but losin' sight of my soul caught up in the hustle, forgettin' the goal.
They applaud when you're winnin', but leave when you fall. In this game of life, I'm givin' it my all.
Character over currency, that's what's real in a world full of fakes, I'm stayin' true to what I feel. In this relentless duel, it's truth I seek,
Not the hollow victory of the strong over the weak.
The world outside may crumble, fortunes may shift,
but a soul that's unyieldin' is the ultimate gift..

My Define Meaning of Love

Love thrives on value, happiness, cherished memories, personal growth, and the profound gift of unconditional acceptance.

At its core, unconditional acceptance flourishes through steadfast devotion, unwavering loyalty, trust that withstands the tests of time, and the honesty that nurtures deep connections, all guided by the firm hand of discipline.

Discipline, in turn, finds its roots in respect, truthfulness, and the serenity that arises when hearts are at peace.

Peace itself hinges on the gentle dance of mutual communication and the warmth of shared smiles.

A smile, that simple yet profound expression, is anchored in a keen sense of humor and the depth of genuine connection.

Being with you has granted me the incredible

fortune to experience all of these elements.
Had our paths not crossed, I can't help but
think that I would be one in a million,
navigating a world without truly grasping
the profound meaning of love.
If fate ever posed the question of who I would
choose in a world of death before dishonor,
your hand is the one I would seek.
Marriage is a sacred honor, and honor
itself is a fundamental pillar of love, which
intertwines with the complexities of
bondage, pleasure, and even pain.

My Ideal Right Type

Let me begin by saying my life has been far from perfect. Shaped by my environment, I learned the essence of hustle before understanding care. No single woman defined respect or commitment for me. Instead, I knew the strength of a firm grip and the unpredictability of conflict. Life handed me nothing, so my survival instinct was to take. My family didn't hold together, and pride kept me from seeking help. Inspired by Kells and Jeezy, I became a go-getter; it was that or face hunger, and nothing comes to those without resources.

My unrestrained actions quickly led to losing my freedom—years swept away, locked in a place where iron is lifted to build gorilla-like strength. I'm not a bad person, nor do I make excuses; I didn't create poverty or isolation, I was born into it and played the hand I was dealt. I grew from a naive boy into a wise man, continuously evolving beyond ignorance to intelligence. Now, I'm wiser, more humble, with intellect reshaping past mistakes. However, I'm not interested in lingering on gossip about my past. I focus on what's right, and unlike Diddy, I don't need just any girl. I seek loyalty—someone who values me through good and bad.

Love, to me, is a blossom that thrives only in the purest soil of unconditional acceptance. "Death before dishonor" guides me as I search for that special woman to share my world. I'm ready to explore love in a space with no punctuation—a seamless journey of pleasure and pain united. I yearn for a woman who'll welcome me under her umbrella, like Rihanna promised, sharing life's rain and shine together.

My Truth

I want somebody to grow old with. Sprite, mind & body I want someone to share my soul with. My last relationship set sail but quickly sank like a battle-ship. When I love, I love hard but when I fall out of love like a paraplegic I don't feel shit, I'm numb to the pain, I can hear the thunder and even though I'm soaking wet I don't feel the rain. Walkin in your truth will cause earthquakes to other people's fairytales, so what I've learned are lessons never have I've taken an L nor do I plan to fail. I ain't perfect. I stumbled, got back up and again I fell, nobody ever taught me anything, I had to figure it out as I go and here I stand still trying to prevail. You either learn a lesson or become the lesson. A wise man told me, life isn't about figuring out it's about living but where will life take you if you don't have that love there to sedate you. Nowa-days nothing is authentic, it's but a mirage, everyone's all for self nobody searching for a real love like Mary J. Blige it's either you do or that love will die. Encanto the candle that burned you allowed it to die now I'm feeling like Jay when he made Song Cry. You don't remember that and I don't remember you...

6/20/23

Navigating Life's Transformations

Priorities in life change when life changes/
Adapt to the shifts, rewrite your pages/

What once seemed vital now fades to the rear/
Clarity emerges, vision sharp and clear/

Chasing dreams that evolve with each twist
and turn/
Lessons learned from bridges that we watch
burn/

Love and loss shape the paths we pursue/
Moments of struggle give birth to what's true/

Time reveals what truly matters most/
Family, passion, memories we host/

No longer bound by superficial aims/
Seeking deeper meaning, igniting new flames/

Embracing growth, welcoming the unknown/
Building futures from seeds we've sown/

Resilient hearts find strength in the change/
Navigating life's journey, we constantly rearrange/

Adapting, thriving, with each passing stage/
Priorities in life change when life changes..

Just like Nipsey, I'm on this #VictoryLap grind,
Chasing the fortune, ditching the fleeting fame,
'Cause the moment you gain that spotlight, you start to feel the shame, they say it's the government, but was it really that dude he slapped?
Man, if this is the price for chasing dreams,
I'm not about that life, I'll pass on those horrific scenes.
You don't need to be a household name,
Just ask around; my hustle's been stamped, with no need for acclaim.
I pen these verses straight from the depths of my soul, why? 'Cause that's the only way I know to stay whole.
Was it Nipsey's time to go? That question

haunts my mind, but I assure you, you'd
never catch me slipping behind.
I might lack the status but in my city, I glide,
always aware, keeping my eyes open wide,
bullets don't discriminate, they don't care
who they claim,
I won't be taken out easily, it's a savage game.
Every day I pray, for my daughter to know no
pain,
So I carry that stick with me, like I've been told
it's my cane.
It's a damn shame that every black man,
reaching for the stars, has to leave behind
their legacy, a heartache that's forever
marred.
It's not just our own brothers we have to fear,
even the ones in power seem to hold a
sneer.
What gives you the audacity to be mad at my
skin?
You've painted us with your history, but still,
we rise from within.
Rest In Peace Trayvon, Tupac, Biggie too,
Malcolm X taken, Nelson Mandela locked
away from view,
Now Nipsey gone such a heavy toll, this isn't
just rap this is my heart, my soul.
Got that nine on my side with two clips ready to
roll, but even stripped of that, I won't let go
of control.
I'm skilled with these hands, just like The Rock
in his prime, cross that line, my friend, and
it's you who'll face the crime.

This ain't a show, ain't no wrestling themes,
It's survival, my life, navigating through these dreams. I haven't slept, not since I heard this news,
Another black king lost, another life we must uproot, kust doesn't sit right, it gnaws at my core,
So I say it loud Rest In Peace, Nipsey forevermore.

Nobody Knows

In the shadows of doubt, where hope seems to fade,
I'm lost in the darkness, my mind's a charade.
Voices whisper doubts in my ear, feedin the darkness, nurturin' fear. I've seen the light flicker, then suddenly hide, in the heart of the struggle, where the shadows reside. Moments of clarity are lost in the storm, tryin' to find warmth where the cold is the norm. Every step feels heavy, every breath a sigh, I'm just a man searchin' for meanin' in a world gone awry. The road's long, and the paths unclear. Can courage be found in the face of fear?
Dreams shatter like glass, cuttin' deep into my soul,
as I wander this path, no longer whole.
The light at the end of the tunnel's a myth,
a cruel joke life plays, leavin' me adrift.

Promises broken, trust turned to dust,
In this life, who can I trust?
The weight of the world on these shoulders I bear,
crushed by the burden, consumed by despair.
Silent screams echo in the halls of my mind,
Tryin' to grasp a hope I can't find.
Emptiness fills the void where love used to be is now but a hollow existence, just driftin' at sea.
Every smile's a mask, every laugh a lie,
Hidin' the turmoil I feel inside. In the mirror's reflection, a soul torn in two,
one side's the warrior, the other subdued.
The future's a question, the past is a scar,
wishin' upon stars that seem so far.
In a war where the casualties are my pleas, I'm battlin' demons alone that no one else sees. I wear a brave face to stand out in the crowd, but in the silence of my mind the pain echoes loud.
Memories haunt like a relentless tide,
washin' away the strength I once had inside.
Dreams turn to nightmares, hauntin' my sleep in a world so shallow I've drowned in the deep. My heart beats heavy with the weight of sorrow,
questionin' if there's any hope for tomorrow.
Hope feels distant, a fadin' illusion,
lost in a sea of endless confusion.
In the silence of night, my fears take flight,
lost in the darkness, far from the light.
Every heartbeat echoes the pain within.

In this battle of life, can I ever win?
As the Angels cover the evil, truth covers the lies,
heavy rain covers the sun, even with your eyes
open you can be blind to the world outside.
Is it ok to cry when you're dyin' inside?

Not Being Afraid to Love Again

When I once knew her, I could've sworn the love we had for one another was pure like the crystalline waters of nirvana or the vibrant blood coursing through the veins of a thoroughbred. Nah, don't get this twisted; the feeling I have for her runs deep through the valleys of Heart, mind, body, and soul. The words honor, love, and loyalty are more than just nouns, verbs, and synonyms to me, just as the earth couldn't blossom without its lush grass, twinkling stars, blazing sun, flowing water, and gentle moon.

Love... it's truly amazing that we shared that once. It seems like just yesterday that I had the honor of breathing life into the rhythm of her heartbeat, experiencing the pleasure of my fantasy. You know what's funny? I'd probably never say it, but she made this man feel complete. Yet here I am, yesterday's echoes fading into the void. I've closed my eyes and awakened from the depths of that slumber, realizing she was never meant to stay. The past is now a haunting shadow in my rearview, my hands are empty, and when I turn around, all that greets me is the chilling embrace of a winter breeze. I find myself trapped in a world woven within another, confined within a cell that houses so many institutionalized minds.

I often ponder, how do I embrace sleep when she's gone? I can't even hold her in my thoughts, yet another side nudges me, whispering that it's simple: just step into her shoes. She cast aside love like a reckless dime pass. Sleep comes easy because life marches on, or maybe I've come to realize that everything that glitters ain't gold. Love is just another overused word, tossed around like hate, frustration, and anger. Nah, even I have trouble believing that.

But I know for a fact that a person will never be on their best behavior under the unflinching gaze of direct eye contact. Damn, it hit me by surprise, like a shadow lurking in the dark that I didn't see coming. My time away wasn't easy, but it wasn't hard either, and every night when the lights dimmed, I saw you. You were that shadow in the dark.

And to think I had her back. I remember once hearing a saying—one I abided by—about letting go. I had to release her without much choice, but will she come back and try to walk into my life again? A chapter that's meant to be shut tightly, sealed off and closed, but somehow lies open, waiting for her to reenact a new beginning.

What type of guy is he? Some might consider him a sucker for love or regard him as less of a man. She used and abused her position, and still here I stand, my heart not on my sleeve, but cradled in the palm of my hand.

I've come to the conclusion that following my pride

instead of my heart defines me as less of a man. So hey, when you've traversed the cycles of love, you understand it's not about being a sucker for love; it's about not fearing to give love a second chance... not being afraid to love again.

Only in America

What kind of country is this? Only in America can the Ku Klux Klan thrive, where white supremacy reigns unchecked. If I raise this peace sign and aim it at a cop, I'm seen as a threat, and it could very well land me unconscious on the pavement. They chant "Black Lives Matter" now, but let's not forget that Black lives have always been relevant. We were the Egyptians first kings and queens before being kidnapped, sold, and forced into slavery. We built this country with our bare hands, just as we constructed the pyramids. It makes you wonder: what did we fail to achieve that the Native Americans did? Here's the answer: we haven't learned to unify as a community, to use our intellect and resilience. Because of that, we don't receive reparations like they do. Instead, we face brutal beatings, unjust incarcerations, and are gunned down mercilessly.

Think about that for a moment, let it sink in. We were brought to America, and we physically built this nation, but let's be real: America isn't a welcoming place for Black skin. I don't consider myself racist, but if a cop shoots one of my kin, turning the other cheek isn't an option; it's an eye for an eye just like the Bible says. So, mark my words: it could drive me to take lethal action.

Only in America do we celebrate Columbus, presidents, memorials, and Independence Day. And let's not forget 9/11, events we're told to remember. But when I speak up about the plight of Black lives, I'm constantly reminded of those antiquated slavery days. Damn America, damn your national anthem, and damn your American flag! They call it the home of the brave and the land of the free, but all I witness is a cycle of murder inflicted upon my people. Six-six-six who's really the mark of the beast? I don't believe in Jesus Christ or his father; in my eyes, to either of them, Black lives don't hold any value. So why should I place my faith in a faith based on a man-made manuscript that disregards our existence?

Oral Sexduction (Your Body)

I want to begin with a gentle kiss, making my way slowly from the top of your head, savoring every strand of your hair. I move tenderly down to your eyelids and then to your earlobes, softly whispering how your beauty captivates and excites me. As I journey further, I envision creating a fountain of shared passion and connection. My fingers trace your neck, lightly moving from shoulder to shoulder, until they find your firm breasts, which I delight in as though discovering a hidden treasure. A volt of electricity courses through us as my tongue caresses your skin, with soft breaths playing upon your sensitive nipples, making them respond eagerly.

I continue down, showering your stomach with tender, passionate kisses, creating a trail that speaks of longing. I pause slightly, teasing, drawing it out as I gently nibble on your pelvis, building anticipation. Spreading your thighs, I give each one the attention they deserve, kissing and caressing each with devotion. Your inviting scent draws me closer, tempting me to dive deeper into your world. As your hips rise, offering yourself to me, I fight the urge to rush, savoring every moment.

I leisurely make my way to your feet, honoring each delicate toe with a kiss and a touch, each sensation driven by my deep affection for you. Slowly, I return to your most intimate place, where my tongue dances upon your sensitive clitoris, softly flicking and exploring, while my hands find their way back to caress your breasts and tenderly fondle your erect nipples.

Lost in your essence, I part your lips with my tongue, entering gently, reveling in the taste of our shared harmony. Your intoxicating moans spur me on as I explore with gentle yet confident strokes. Overwhelmed with passion, I continue until your body trembles, gasping for air, until the crescendo leaves us both breathless.

Finally, I rise above you, gazing into your eyes, and kiss you deeply, our tongues intertwining like magnets drawn together, sharing a moment of profound intimacy and love.

Overcoming Struggles

Comin' from where I come from, we have to
beat the streets, beat the system, beat
racism and poverty.
Ten years I held it in and not shed a tear. Had a
story locked up, thought it was normal
they'd leave us here.
I was 19 when I seen a man thrown to his death
from the fourth tier, his last breath lost to
the depths.
Lost in the struggle, every days a test to
survive,
I grind hard tryin to never let my dreams take a
dive, though at times I feel mentally
deprived.
Life can hit hard like a wrecking ball. You
either rise or you fall, take a step or you
crawl.
I've watched friends fall victim to the same

cursed cycle, locked up or laid out, living suicidal.
I moved differently, and knew I had to fight.
Radiohead life taught me to rock and roll,
survive the war within, it was either that or watch my life fold.
Dodged bullets and dreams that crumbled to dust,
watched hope slip away, lost in words and mistrust,
But in the darkest nights, when my vision went blind, I saw a future shining, though it seemed out of mind.
They never gave us a chance, wrote us off quick,
said we'd amount to nothing, just another statistic,
but I refused to be a product of the district,
I made my own path, broke free from the mystic.
Cops have no discipline, killing Black men out of fear, judging the worth of a life by the color they fear. And the unjust system we live in doesn't even care, they turn a blind eye pretending it's all fair.
Every scar on my soul's a mark I can't erase.
Most days all I felt was pain, numb like my veins bled novocaine.
Fighting wars in the dark, quiet and deranged,
but in time I burned through the wreckage, lit a match and turnt my rage into flames.
Transformed the pain into heat, let the damage ignite, wore the ashes as armor, each fracture fueled the fight.

Now I stand tall, the streets couldn't bend me,
learned from the struggle, no chains can bind me,
I'm living proof that the system couldn't design me,
risen above it all, they no longer define me.
For the ones without a voice I write our stories in blood. The only path to success is breaking the chains they forged, comin' from where I come from, there's strength in the gorge.
This is for the streets, for the silenced and weak,
for the dreams that were crushed, for the voices that squeak, but in our silence, there's a roar that will peak. I share my story now, no longer chained by fear of the pain that shaped me, the dues paid dear.
Comin' from where I come from, we never disappear, we just keep rising, despite the cards we were dealt here.

Pain

Pain is when you feel like you want to die. That feeling you feel inside that makes you want to do nothing but cry. It's DMX slipping, falling and can't get up.
It's when you want to be alone in the dark and rock yourself to sleep.
Pain is when you don't want to talk to anyone and just want to be left alone.
Pain is when you grow up being abused mentally and physically. It's when you've only heard your mother express her love for you from a prison call from the penitentiary.
Pain is when you can't shake the ptsd. It's when you can't run from the memories of your mother locking you in a closet to entice her male companion and smoke crack.
Pain is when you meet your father for the first

time and him giving you an excuse as to why he turned his back. It's when 2pac said his anger wouldn't let him feel for a stranger.
People say there's beauty in pain but it's not.
It's when you want to strangle someone until they feel what pain is. It's when you're in pain but try to convince yourself you're not.
People say pain feels terrific when it doesn't. If it did, why do gunshot wounds still hurt when it rains?
Some say pain is stressful and they're right.
It's when you cut yourself and say "I'm alright"
They say pain is relaxing, well it's not. Having to take medication to rid the pain says a lot.
My pain ain't your pain but you can see what I've endured when you look in my eyes no I'm not that serious I just harbor a lot of pain inside. You don't know pain if you've never contemplated suicide.
Pain is losing someone to a violent death then America turn around and glorify the murderer by putting out a doc'.
Pain I've been through enough to know if you don't find the right help like the breath you take the pain won't stop..

10/16/22

Picture Window

The saying goes that a picture speaks a thousand words – peer through my picture window, and you'll discover there's far more than meets the eye. Beyond the lifeless rose, the solitary cuff, the whisper of seduction, the hourglass, and the shattered ink pen amidst scattered papers, lies a deeper truth.

Look through my picture window, and you'll uncover Lovelorn, a wilted rose that speaks of a love lost, its petals a testament to companionship deprived of warmth and understanding. Each withered petal echoes the laughter that once filled my days, replaced now by silence.

Gaze deeper into my picture window, and you'll find Induration, a lone cuff resting in stark isolation, a symbol of a heart that has grown cold and unyielding. This physical restraint mirrors the emotional barriers I've constructed, forged in the fires of solitary confinement, a fortress built from desperation and fear.

Shift your gaze, and beyond my picture window, you'll see Rogue. It's not just a seductive act; it's the ghost of women who've danced through my past, forever imprinted in my memory. Mischievous and enchanting, they haunt my thoughts, reminding me of what was, and what can never be again.

In that same breath, peer through my picture window, what awaits you is Forlorn, an hourglass frozen in time, counting down ten agonizing years of sadness and solitude. Each grain of sand represents my isolation, the relentless ticking a reminder of family left behind, of empty spaces that once held laughter and love.

And then, there lies Jim Dandy, a busted pen and ink-stained scraps, a vivid testament to my struggle to articulate my existence. Each scattered sheet holds fragments of my soul, my thoughts, and dreams spilled onto paper, an attempt to create something brilliant out of chaos, to manifest my life in a world that feels increasingly distant.

So, look closely through my picture window, and you will see me, here I am, here I stand, strengthened by the shadows of turmoil, pain, neglect, hatred, and doubt. These scars have not defeated me; they have woven the fabric of my resilience, reminding me of the strength that lies within, even when the world outside remains unforgiving.

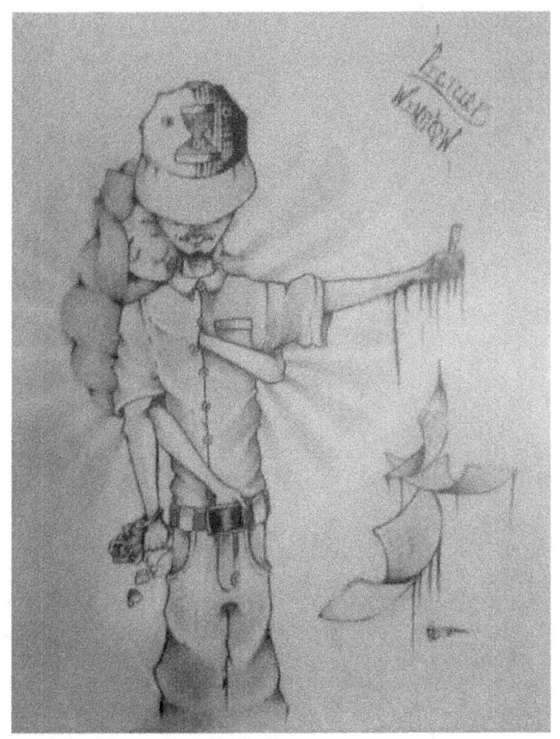

Pieces of a Purpose

A mind exposed to a new idea never returns to its original condition though the lack of faith in oneself deprives most individuals holdin' them back from the obvious.

Out of many I am but one person who has fail to plan, learnin' and teachin' myself and return expectin' somethin'.....out of life.

Pieces of a purpose dwell within the essence of thought and character, thought and character are one. Character can only manifest and discover itself through environment and circumstance. When thought coincides with purpose there can be an intelligent result.

The sophisticated more intellectual terms that defines "Being" are mortal, life, existence – to be. We're called human beings for which means we are structured and made to be somethin'.

I think therefore I exist; I exist through the
manifestations of my thoughts.
Out of many I am but one person, one link to
the pieces of a purpose..

Poetic Expression

I'm a poet, not a rapper, a painter with words
craftin' visions and dreams in vibrant strokes
that blur, if not my lifestyle, a depiction of
what I've seen. A canvas of emotions,
flowing colors so serene.
Nowadays, rappers rap to be heard, chasin'
fame,
but I write every line superb, like a weapon in
the game.
Cuttin' through the noise with the sharpest
verbs,
my pen spills ink like a river, with currents that
disturb.
Each verse is a chill, like winter's bitin' air, my
Illmatic lines cascade, timeless and rare.
I paint a picture with words so divine,
like constellations in the night how they
perfectly aligned.
My thoughts go deeper than a scalpel on skin,

carvin' truths in the silence, that's where I begin.
I don't spit; I recite a head full of flames like ghost rider, turnin' darkness to light.
I weave tapestries of thoughts, intricate and fine,
like threads of silk, how my emotions intertwine.
No chains, no gold, just the weight of my soul,
Each rhyme is a reflection, with raw truths as my goal.

Profound Intimacy Beyond the Physical

Many men seek brief embraces, yet rarely do they find
a connection that resonates through heart, body, and mind. They speak of fleeting whispers, charms gone too soon, while the beauty of deep love is like a lost rune.

True intimacy needs more than surface allure,
in whispers and touches, it must feel secure.
A gaze that speaks volumes, a kiss that's sincere,
a touch that says "I'm here and will never disappear."

She might reach for him just to fill her own need,
overlooking his soul, where rich emotions plead.

He longs for a connection that's real and
complete,
in mind, body, and spirit, where true lovers
meet.

Engaging talk that sparks their hearts into
flight,
foreplay that draws souls closer, into the night.
She must feel his whispers, know when he
dreams,
and cherish those moments where love forever
gleams.

Nights are his solace, memories in his heart
kept,
weaving wonder into dreams, where passions
are swept.
A touch on his neck, a map to his desires,
a love that burns brightly, kindles unseen fires.

Holding him near, in a bond forged tight,
tenderness unmatched, like the stars in the
night.
His arms drawing her in, a homecoming
embrace,
a melding of energies in a sacred, shared space.

Her movements reflect his inner melody,
creating a rhythm of love that's heavenly.
Masculine, Feminine, in balance they find,
an intimate connection that touches the mind.

When warmth surrounds and hearts are made whole,
together they craft a journey touching each other's soul

Reimagining History and Society's What If's

What if a bullet birth life into you instead of taking it out?
What if we never grew old and any and all diseases – cancers exist?
What if cars like the one from "Back to The Future" were sold right at the lot of your local dealership?
What if our way of livin' was similar to the one in the movie "5th Element" flyin cars through the sky and every meal you ate was a space pack?
What if Bush would've signed a bill to bring slavery back, what if the war was staged right here in America not over in Afghanistan or Iraq?
What if 9/11 was an attack on the white house instead of the twin tower buildings?
What if Kennedy would've seen it all like déjà vu and had the opportunity to have a few

words to say to the assassin before he was set to die?
What if Ali would've fought that war? It's a war going on right now unjustly murder on blacks. It's a war goin on right now. What are those people dyin for, for a country whose was in cahoots with the 9/11 attack started a war but wouldn't die for you?
What if the Million Man March was a miscalculation and the estimate was a billion?
What if the holiday Thanksgiving was created by black folks instead of pilgrims?
What if what Emmitt Till said never got back or when they came searchin for son his family was armed with enough firearms to erase a small state off the U.S. map?
What if the 1954 Supreme Court case Brown vs. The Board of Education was a discrepancy involving nine whites instead of blacks?
What if racism was just a figment of our minds but for real what if it wasn't blacks but white folks affected by genocide.
What if the Ten Commandments was eleven and that eleventh commandment read it's a sin to lack intelligence and you don't have to be a lawyer or a doctor – Martin Luther King but to become something in life was mandatorily relevant.
What if life came with buttons like pause and rewind, and right before the shots rang what if 2Pac pressed rewind and he hopped

out the car, gave Suge dap and saw him off
with a peace sign?
What if B.I.G saw it coming out the corner of
his eye and pressed pause to buy enough
time to reach for twin tech nines?
What if everyone except Aaliyah would've
died? What if that plane crash was but an
illusion that played a trick on all of our
minds?
What if Left Eye never took that drive? What if
she ran out of gas hitched hiked and was
given a ride?
What if Jam Master J and Big L were still alive?
What if Diddy was deported instead of Shyne?
What if I could give back every bit of my time
and my father was a man that didn't walk
out of my life but instead taught me some-
thing other than what I learned from
Father Time. Like what if hurt people never
hurt people and we all grew up on how to
love not some growing up on how to
survive. What if I was featured on that
track "What If" with the brothers Jadakiss
and Nas?
What if Mc Hammer was still rich and Mike
Tyson prevented Don Kind and Robin
Givens from taking him for his chips? What
if he was sharp with his mind like he was
with his fist?
What if O.J. Simpson was Bill O'Reilly and that
female that was murdered was Nancy
Grace? What if it was a court appointed

lawyer? What if Johnny Cochran never accepted his case?
Why is it growing up in poverty that life is hard? Why do so many white kids try to emulate a style like ours, like our way of living is cool? The life isolation and poverty inflicted on me I wouldn't recommend any kid to be dealt those cards because the way I was born and raised is not a façade.
Why is it that out of every race blacks are a majority of the folks behind bars?
Why is suffering the defined meaning to survive?
Why is marijuana an earth grown plant that could get you sat down in a cell for a long time? But if a white cop kills an unarmed black man the justice system turns blind.
What if like the wind our problems were able to be blown away instead of being something so hard to deal with?
What if "what if's" was something that could manifest into existence?

Revolution Forged in Pain

I was given this world, I didn't make it,
Went and fell in love with the skin that I'm in
but I ain't create it,
Was once called a nigger but couldn't fathom
how one could be filled with such hatred.
I mean, what did we do?
You said freeze, put my hands up, but still, you
pulled your gun and commenced to shoot.
How could you hate me? I was enslaved, beaten,
and chained, not you. What did we do?
Tried to breathe free but you kneeled on my
neck,
Bled on these streets while my soul screamed for
respect.
My ancestors' cries echo in the night,
Hoping for a dawn where we rise from this
plight.
Can't kill something that's ready to die,
Injustice lit fires, now it's time to reply.

From the roots of pain, a legacy grew,
We carry the scars, but we march on through.
Can't silence our voices, can't dim our light,
We've endured the darkness, now we claim our right.
Through tears and the struggle, our spirits don't break, for every life lost, a revolution we make..

Ride Wit' Me

Ride with me, let's journey to a realm where the harsh realities of life fade into oblivion, a sanctuary where no gangs linger, where disputes are not settled with guns or blades, but with boxing gloves in the ring. Here, every problem is met with the raw power of fists, and when the final bell rings, it's all love. Miscommunication, envy, and bloodshed will be left behind in the squared circle.

Ride with me to a place where drugs are nonexistent, no needles or pipes, where the only highs come from the intoxicating feelings of honor, loyalty, and love. Imagine a land where stores sell no nicotine or liquor, a haven free from foul language and ignorance, untainted by the scourges of exploitation or disease, a place where the people are untouched by the shadow of AIDS.

Ride with me to a world where race and the color of your skin are mere shades in a beautiful tapestry, where every ethnicity stands on equal ground. Here, police harassment doesn't stalk Hispanics, Latinos, or Black individuals; instead, there is understanding and respect.

Ride with me to a haven of higher learning, a realm where education is a birthright, free from monetary burdens. Picture a place where graduation comes with the promise of a bright future, where we learn not just from textbooks but by sharing knowledge with one another.

Ride with me to a place where tomorrow is always promised, where truth reigns supreme over all things. Envision a realm without oppressive laws, where the notion of "protect and serve" transcends into justice that flows down from the heavens. Walk these streets without a hint of paranoia gnawing at your mind; feel the peace as you stroll through your neighborhood. Come ride with me, take the passenger seat in this journey of dreams.

Seasons Of Emotion

A shroud of moisture hangs in the air, like the heavy fog of a Southern California morning that hasn't tasted tears in years. Yet, behind the portals of my eyes, a bustling rain forest teems with uncried sorrow, each droplet echoing the silent heartbreak within. When the rain descends, it strikes like a gunshot, sending ripples of pain straight through my heart. And during the snows, this heart of mine, already heavy, is enveloped by a glacier of ice, colder than the ocean where the Titanic once sailed, each layer freezing the warmth of joy beneath.

In the darkness, the unbearable emotions twist and writhe, concealed behind the windows of my soul. The moon casts a gentle glow, illuminating the surface—a mere hint of the tempest that rages within the accolades of my mind. Each glimmer of light serves only as a fleeting clue to the emotional storm brewing just beneath the surface, waiting for a moment to break free.

Seeking Forgiveness and Strength from Loss

I carry a burden heavy, it pulls at my heart,
I look to the sky, wondering where we go when we part?
Is there truly another side that we can see?
My grandmother's gone, and it haunts me, silently.
No chance for goodbyes, or to make amends,
While I served my time, the real world transcends.
Her absence cuts deeper than missing my kids,
forgiveness flows slowly for the wrongs that she did.
Our last moments replay like a film in my mind,
"Get from 'round my crib," harsh words left behind.
Just weeks after that, at the age of sweet sixteen,

handcuffed, I stood where the dark shadows gleaned.
Transferred to prison, a sentence of three and a half,
locked in a cage, but still seeking a path.
Though she wasn't the best, my heart still learns,
from pain comes the strength, from ashes hope burns.

Seeking Light in a World of Shadows

All I hear is rain, rain poundin' against the rooftop, a chaotic dance upon my windowpane, poolin' into shimmerin' puddles that splash and settle as I step from my vehicle, my black hoodie drawn tight against the chill. UnderArmor clings to my chest like an unwaverin' shield, and I can't help but wish that countless souls could find their solace under armor; perhaps then the rain wouldn't pour so fiercely, cleansin' the streets of both blood and chalk, lifting the shroud of despair where lost souls could rise and roam free.

RAs I pull back my hood and snapback, I stand undeterred by the relentless downpour, liftin' my face to the tumultuous sky, a burden of confusion sinkin' deep into my heart. I close my eyes, envisionin' what it would be like to share just one more precious moment with you. So many of you rest in eternal peace, while others remain trapped, never to return home from the cold, unyieldin' walls of the penitentiary or the distant, barren fields of Afghanistan.

Grand Rapids, Michigan, December—the
weather…Gray.
The rain…Thick.
Humanity…Hopeless.

I awaken to find depression pressin' down on me like a heavy shroud, dark thoughts swirlin' like storm clouds in my mind. Yet, through it all, I promise to persevere; I will ensure that the sun breaks through once more.

Sex Chronicles

Does it really pour when it rains? If that's true, it mirrors my desire for you.

Heart rate accelerates as I pull you close, bodies warming, passion brews. Our kisses ignite like thunder in the storm's view.

Exploring your body, every inch a map, my fingers trace the routes.

Your body's whispers, I listen intently, addressing more than just your doubts.

Showing you what I mean when the sky turns dark blue, treating this moment like it's priceless, every second feels brand new.

Seeing you standing here before me, water dripping from your curls, draped in just a towel, your allure's profound.

I scoop you by your ass and sit you on the table, grab your hair, tilt your head back, adorn your neck with bites and kisses.

Alexa play, Take You Down by Chris Brown

You spread your legs, I touch your clit, my own desire flows as I gently caress, suck and lick your hardened nipples, a pinch here and there, our lust grows.

On one knee, surrendering completely, lost in your taste I french kiss your pussy, tongue on clit, I pause to build the urge, to dive deep inside you, as anticipation shows. The electricity, igniting our desire, our bodies burning in this untamed fire,

every breath taken, only lifting us higher.

I can feel the build up as you tremble ready to explode.

Pushing my head back. Suddenly you take control.

Alexa play, Needed Me by Ri Ri

Easing from the table. You greet me as I stand, kiss and bite my lip, pain's pleasure entwines.

Licks down my chest all the while you stare me in the eyes, reaches my dick, our strong pulses aligned. With your tongue you tease the tip, then take me fully, wrapped like a lollipop. Spit runs down your chest, deep throating, making yourself choke, but you don't stop.

Breathing heavy, touching, kissing. I lay down into a deep stroke. Squirting, creaming, water flowing, you're my boat, let me steer you drenched in lust, waves crashing, let the passion guide me deeper in you.

Moaning, arching, lost in lust, our bodies climb, your skin on mine, electric shock, our hearts beat in perfect time.

Eyes locked, intensity rises, you say "turn me over, smack my ass, go berserk" Yelling out, " deeper"

I'm the conductor, you're the perk.

Pulsating, can't contain, busting, waters needed, to contain the sweat and heavy breathing. Our climax shared, bodies spent, love's law.

I carry you to the shower, back against the wall, legs

around my waist as the water flows, fluently dancing off our entangled bodies like niagara falls.

You pull me closer. I go deeper and deeper and deeper, attempting to align every inch of me with your spine. Kissing my earlobe in every breath you sighs:

"Does it really pour when it rains? If that's true, the way I crave you is the same"

Every touch, every glance, ignites a flame,
I wake to find it's all in vain.
Just a vision, a dream I can't sustain.

Sex, Love and Vices

In the moonlight, our shadows intertwine body
to body l caress and hold you tight,
every touch the chills down your spine ignites
the night.
Lust's a game we play, the stakes rise high,
love and vices, we're living on the edge.
In a haze of passion, we dance, hearts collide,
temptation's pull, can't resist the rising tide.
Champagne dreams and velvet skies, we fly,
Lost in moments where the truth and lies belie.
Ecstasy and sin, we tread that fine line,
In the heat of desire, our worlds combine.
Burning bright, yet knowing it's all a vice,
In love's embrace, we pay the price.
Whispers linger, fingers trace our skin,
In this game of hearts, who'll lose, who'll win?
Candlelight flickers, casting shadows wide,
In every kiss, another secret hides.
Seduction's art, painted in hues of night,

We chase the dawn, avoiding morning's light.
Our souls entwined, caught in lust's embrace,
Navigating a path through time and space.
Forbidden fruit tastes sweeter, so we indulge,
In each other's arms, we find and lose control.
Pleasure and pain, two sides of our coin,
In this dance of love, our bodies join.
Deception's whisper, but truth's glaring face,
In this labyrinth, we both find our place.
Night's allure, a promise of delight,
With every breath, we fan the fire's light.
Hearts on fire, yet so cold inside,
We ride the waves, no shore in sight.
Our passions peak, then ebb away,
In love's deep sea, we choose to stay.
Fragile and fierce, our vices show,
In the moonlight's glow, our secrets grow.
Lost in each other, we find our way,
In love and vices, night turns to day..

Silent Struggles

In the silence of night, I wrestle with fate,
at war within myself, where peace seems out of date.
I suffer without words, don't let complaints fly.
Even in victory I still feel like a part of me die.

Pieces of my essence erode away with each round,
In the midst of my silent struggle, I fight without sound.
Each triumph feels like a forlorn game,
winning the battle but losing the same.

Barely keeping my head over the tide's crest,
living on the edge, is an uninvited test.
The water whispers with threats they be hard to ignore,
drawing me down to this murky ocean floor.

When you sip from release, thinking respite is found,
careful, 'cause indulgence might make you drown.
I'm dancing on the precipice, a delicate sway,
fighting currents that's pulling me in the opposite way.

My thoughts are storms that rage in quiet disguise,
words left unspoken escapes through my tired eyes.
The silence is a friend that knows every scar,
in battles unseen, you often lose who you are.

Despite the turmoil, I put on a mask show,
the worlds unaware of the combat below.
It's hard to keep steady when the waves overwhelm,
navigating troubled waters and I'm at the helm.

The weight of my burdens, invisible, intense,
each moment a battle in silent pretense.
Though calm above, there's chaos that's underneath,
striving to breathe while the depths try to sheath.

Something to think about

Home is where the heart truly resides.
Love lives within where comfort abides.
Being rich is a mindset, a powerful start,
while being poor often stems from the heart.
From something as small as a fleeting thought,
You produce what you consume; negativity's caught. If darkness fills your mind, it takes hold and stays, sowing seeds of despair that cloud brighter days. In gritty streets, profound lessons are drawn, shaping desires from dusk til dawn.
You become the thoughts that you choose to feed,
planting doubt or the hopeful seed.
Amidst the grind, with struggles that bind,
strength emerges, through the chaos you find.
Seek out the light, let your spirit impart.
For home is where you always place your heart.

Stay Alive

What's purpose without being, what's being without livin'?
If we live to die, what's the meaning to existin'?
Life's essence lies in more than the breaths we keep givin' in the choices we make, and the truths we're revealin'.
Purpose finds its roots in the paths we're carvin',
In the love we share, and the dreams we're starvin'.
Being transcends just existing in form, it's in the storms we weather, and the norms we transform.
Livin' isn't just survival, it's the light in our eyes,
It's the highs and the lows, and the ties that we prize.
To live is to grow, to seek and to strive,

for meanin' in the journey, not just stayin'
alive.

Strength Amidst Life's Turmoil

I've felt pain but never bruised,
been broken before, yet I refuse to lose.

Misunderstood in all that I say,
life tried to change me, but I found my way.

Though bruised, I rise and still standing tall,
shattered pieces but like that Great Wall of China my spirit won't fall. Life can manipulate feelings and thoughts, but my core beliefs are unchanged. Life can bend the path of my journey, but my destination remains the same.

Love reigns supreme above all that's wrong,
in a world that's deranged where chaos is strong.
Society's shadows may cloud what is right,
yet my morals remain, like stars in the night.

Wise men may stumble while fools wear a
crown,
knowledge forced through walls can still drag
you down.
Being smart is a label, as is being naive,
but my heart knows the truth; I refuse to
believe.

Life may try to shift you, like tides on the sand,
but the essence of you is what will always
stand.
Your morals may change all cleaned and
renewed,
as life teaches lessons in ways that are crude.

Embrace all the battles, let them shape who you
are,
for in the storm's chaos, you shine like a star.

Suicide Thoughts

Have you ever thought about death so much that you see a dark silhouette in your peripheral vision, but when you turn, it disappears? Or have you ever dealt with so much pain inside, alone, that the agony makes you want to die sometimes? When rolling out of bed and driving, you turn the music up loud to drown out the suicidal voices in your head, telling you to slide into oncoming traffic. It might get you closer, but how would you explain that to God? I don't believe in religion, so both heaven and hell to me are just a facade.

Have you ever sat alone in the dark, naked on your living room floor, your back against the couch, with a gun in hand? Not Russian roulette, this is a fully loaded clip. If I pulled that trigger, maybe my thoughts would reveal a Picasso of what goes on in my mind. Blind when I close my eyes, all I can see is my daughter's cry, and what about my other kids I'd be leavin' behind? When I think about it, tears flow like Billie Eilish's ocean eyes as I write, smudgin' the ink.

My grandmother died from alcoholic depression, spendin' her days at the bottom of an empty bottle. I hiccup, then wonder what she would think of me now. There's a cure for everything, but without a drug, how do you help someone battlin' PTSD? Sometimes I close my eyes and wish I could never awaken from sleep. A wise man once told me that even the blind can lead, but they will never know the path. To see the future, you must not open doors to your past.

I beg to be understood every time I show my wrath, confidin' in my ex. Her response was quick and blunt: "You'll be fine." It hurt, but how could I expect anyone else to understand even half of what I feel? No one knows or understands the thoughts in my head or the strength I need daily just to get out of bed, just to open my eyes. Take a look past my smile and personality; look past the disguise. Now, ask yourself, have you ever wanted to die?

survivor's remorse

I'm from where niggas feud for land they'll never own where they raise hell, waste shells and duck baby mamas but rarely escape jail. I remember Kevin, always ablaze, caught up in that rush, back when everyone would swarm the same ride just to grab a quick sale, always on high alert at the first sight of flashing lights, it was every man for himself. Years passed, and tragedy struck; a fiend's blade took my dog down in the middle of a deal. These streets have claimed the lives of my homie Nate and my boy Rovel, leaving scars that never heal.

It's a painful truth, but there are moments I wish some of my brothers had stayed locked away; at least then they'd still be breathing instead of resting beneath the earth, where shadows dwell. No souls behind vacant eyes, only remnants of what once was, a lifeless body remaining. Numbness resonates all I feel is a haunting survivor's guilt, as if I've seen too much, lost too much, and it's drained my ability to care. I'm from a world where honesty vanishes under oath, but deception flourishes freely amidst the chaos.

Pooky got 17 for his first slip-up; he won't taste freedom again until he's around 45. I spoke to him just the other day, he seemed hopeful until he revealed that his young homie, set to come home this past July, was stabbed; he died choking on his blood, left to rot in a cell with a lifer as his fate sealed tight.

I'm from a realm where twelve strangers wield the power to decide your destiny. They hit him with 28, but after subtracting the 15 he'll still owe 13 years to the state; that's a 28-year sentence and not telling if they'll let'em go on his early release date.

Some of us received a winning hand, while others were pushed off the porch, forever haunted, learning to navigate life encased in the weight of survivor's remorse.

Tales from a Concrete Jungle

A Bad Boy in the clip is 112, Lifestyle of The Poor & Dangerous I keep a Big L & I don't even smoke The Chronic but lately I been feeling like it's Me Against The World, and All Eyez on Me, see my Ambitionz Az a Ridah has me Starin' Through My Rearview screaming Hail Mary as if I'm trapped in 36Chambers prepared and Ready to Die but only Kamikaze style I refuse to be taken alive, the bible say reincarnation so I ain't stressing it I'll be Born Again. I take you back when I was State Property level VI for years in the hole three days with nothing to eat or swallow but tears, can you imagine what it's like 9 months straight confined to a cell or you witness a man get stabbed his blood splatter yo shirt and they try to frame you because you wouldn't tell, 2012 they put caution tape up that young boy was put in there with a lifer and got raped in that cell, the system is like Bishop in Juice, it don't give a fuck about you, Rahim or Steel. Marshall Law it's all a numbers game if you black they'll do whatever it takes to keep you under their will. I speak The

Truth, like Sigel said What ya Life Like, where I'm from Guerrilla Warfare it's a jungle, all I know is Juvenile Hell project buildings, Mudra Muzik and crack sales, loyalty is like wifi a bad connection and trust will get you killed only trust nowadays that's sacred is on a dollar bill and for that Ghetty Green we bear arms no bear palms get porridge. I witness my uncle play a wheelchair from the fragment of a bullet shell. My homie lost his life a year after his blood stained & sat in the cloth of my passenger seat, dedicated to the streets, Jay Reed he was In Too Deep, I didn't make it to the funeral but homie rest in peace. Do you know what it's like being broke and a fein pull up on you and all you got is a bag full of soap, what you know about puttin' bread in the microwave lettin it harden then you squeeze oral gel on it, sellin' feins candle wax and tryin' to haul ass before they double back, I still remember the night that drug addict showed up to where my aunt live, yeah we got the blood off the porch but a black light would've revealed that, we were just kids at the time probably eleven and twelve livin' life like AC/DC, on a Highway to Hell, poverty stricken my mother never acted as nor presented a role model so I ain't believe in tomorrow like a deadbeat fathers broken promise leaving you hollow.

The Cost of Chasing Clout

Wealth is silent, rich is loud and poor is flashy.
Money's the new god, pussy is currency, attention is worth more than honesty currently
Influence the new gold, fame the new throne,
Selling our souls for a moments a loan,
In the age of the screen, where the image is king,
Chasin' the clout that the followers bring.
Invisible chains, our desires enslaved,
Values traded for likes and praise,
Truth buried deep, in a sea of facade,
Authenticity lost in the digital charade.
Lambo's and mansions, they flex for the gram',
Shallow connections, built on the scam,
The hustle is glam, the struggle's unseen,
behind every post, a silent scream.
Chasin' a dream, but we're stuck in the loop,
Material wealth, but our spirits are duped,
Currency's virtual, value's a lie,

In a world where the shallow and empty fly high.
Fakin' the real, for a fleetin' applause,
Lost in the scroll, for a moment of pause,
Empty ambition, in the guise of success,
the soul's the cost, but we'll never confess.
From the highs of a screen, to the lows of the night,
Our hearts hollow out, in the digital light,
seekin' the real, but it's buried beneath.
In this kingdom of greed, we've forgotten belief..

The Crown of Respect:

WHY LOYALTY OUTSHINES LOVE

I rather have respect than love because love
really don't mean jack, love is just a feeling,
you can love somebody and still stab'em in
the back.
It doesn't really take much to love, because you
can love somebody just by being attached.
Loyalty is an action, you can love me or hate
me and still have my back.
Love is like the wind, it comes and goes as it
pleases, but respect stays solid, even when
everything freezes. Respect is a foundation,
it's the ground beneath my feet, it's the code
that we live by, it's what makes life
complete.
Love can be a weapon, a sharp and twisted
blade,
but respect is a fortress, where trust is never
betrayed.
I've seen love turn sour, watched it fade into the

night, but respect stands firm through every single fight.
You can say you love me, but words are just air.
Show me respect, let me know you truly care.
Love can be selfish, wantin' more than it should,
respect gives freely, understandin' what's good.
I've walked through the fire, felt the burn of love's sting, but respect was my shelter, a knight with a strong wing.
Love is a gamble, a game of win or lose.
Respect is a promise, a bond that we choose. In the end, when the world turns its back it's the respect that holds steady, keepin' everything intact.
Love is a moment, a spark in the dark.
Respect is a beacon, always hittin' the mark.
You can keep your love, if it's empty and hollow,
I'll take respect, a path I'm proud to follow.
So here's to the ones who understand what I mean,
for respect is the king, and love is the queen.
Together they balance, but respect leads the way,
a guidin' star, in the night and day..

The fire anthem against systemic oppression

They say, "In God we trust," but I find no faith
at all, each man's created equal? Not for us;
no, it's a cruel downfall.
You'll never hear me utter "swear to God," in
despair.
The same ones who shackled, murdered, and
laid us bare, expect us to believe they care?
Systematic oppression lingers, it's a rigged
game we play, justice paraded as hope,
mere illusions on display.
Generations crushed beneath the weight of
crafty deceit, strugglin' for freedom, yet
they tighten the noose, instead of a hanging
us with ropes they're now riddling us with
bullets leaving us dead in the street.
Redlining carved our neighborhoods, poverty's
cruel design, black schools starved of fund-
ing, where potential withers like a vine.
Pipelines to prisons, futures lost and dreams

concealed, fighting for survival in a battle-field so skewed.
Economic chasms yawning wide, wealth gaps deeply entrenched,
They preach of equality while building walls, clearly entrenched.
Healthcare denied, as they rake in profits from the pain, politicians spin their web, thriving off our strain.
But we rise, unbreakable, defyin' the chains they cast, unitin' in our struggle, fueled by dreams that will outlast.
We shatter the shackles, rewrite the fate they dictate, tesistin' their dominance, and boldly refusing to placate.

The Fragile Web of Truth

Sometimes, the simplest choice is to weave a web of deception lying to oneself or to that one you cherish. To lie to oneself is an act of self-doubt, a betrayal of self-esteem, a denial of the spirit within. My own heart bears the shame of these truths; I've deceived myself, shackled by insecurities and the pain of self-abandonment. In relationships, I've danced in circles, running back and forth until the trust bestowed upon me became stained, corrupted.

These facades, crafted not out of malice but fear, were never intended to leave her heart shattered and bruised. The coldness that seeped into my actions wasn't who I am, but rather a shield I held up against the world. I thought I was safeguarding her from the harsh reality, yet in my blindness, I failed to see that what lingers in the shadows will always, eventually, find a way to shine bright. It wasn't she who lost me; it was I who lost her, allowing her to slip away burdened by the weight of unmet expectations when all she needed was my hand to help her stand tall.

I am but a man, one of many lost souls born into this chaotic world. I did not choose the rough road I walk, but the journey I've undertaken has left me isolated, stripped of armor, vulnerable to the elements. I loved with a fierceness that flickered with uncertainty, playing her heart like a melancholic saxophone, each note spilling forth echoes of sorrow.

All men are creatures of habit, often drawn to the very actions that lead us astray. Have you ever truly lost someone? I mean, really felt the weight of silence where words once danced, wishing desperately for one more chance to reach out, only to find them gone before you could muster the courage? That ache is a haunting reminder of the fragility of connection, the moments we let slip through our fingers like grains of sand.

The Hand That Feed You

Don't ever bite the hand that feeds you, that's disrespectful. But if what's in the hand deceives you, be skeptical. See, loyalty ain't blind, it's earned through respect when trust turns to dust, got to cut that check, the best way to off a snake you start at the neck, can't break bread with everybody some niggas hiss when you ain't lookin' they shed skin in the dark, but act straight when you cookin'.

That hand might come with promises that everything you touch will turn to gold, but what you didn't know is them chains come with an attribute to buy yo soul. The devil could be somebody close to you. Y'all seen Blow, every business associate ain't yo friend cause when you cash that check, it's your soul that he lookin' to spend. They say gratitude is key, but what if it's a trap?

You gotta ask yourself, is it love or a slap?

Heart's be full of venom, but they words be sweet.

That's a wolf in sheep's clothin', deceivin' your heartbeat. So don't ever bite the hand, that hand will choke you and feed you lies, but don't let it provoke you. It's better to starve in the truth than feast on a lie, all bullshit aside. Sometimes it's easier to cut ties and walk away with yo pride.

Cause when the feast is a famine, and the table's a cage you might find yourself turnin yo hunger to rage.

The Heart's Cycle of Pain and Healing

Like a transplant I gave you my heart and didn't ask for it back, I wouldn't have needed a flashlight. I would have found you in the dark but what I didn't know was that your agenda was to use me from the start. Because of you now it's like I love 'em then breakin' they heart, seems like I'm only good at the breakin' up part.

Hurt people hurt people, that's the cycle we're trapped in. What turned you into a venomous assassin?

Your smile was a dagger, and your words were like poison.

Promises shattered like glass, left me broken. You allowed me to treat you as more than a friend but shortly after went m.i.a just to come back into my life, turn around and do it again. You played with my sanity, your

knavery behavior left me in ruins, a heart in need of mendin' and affection. The pain became my shield, now I'm inflictin' the same, breakin' hearts on replay like a never-ending game.
Your touch was a spell, a hypnosis I now cast onto other females. I've built walls around my heart, keeping out potential lovers. Ice melts, my heart is on the same level as the devil when he was banished from heaven to hell.

Hurt people hurt people, it's the curse we inherit
wounds left open, never healin , only sharin it.
You was the spark, ignitin my inner fire of rage.
Now every woman I've touched unintentionally has felt the remnants of that cage. Theater director and I was just another auditioner on your heartless stage.
I learned the art of betrayal, perfected it well
promises made in the night, by mornin they'd fell, told myself it's just survival, nothin more to tell
though deep down I knew I was castin that same spell on the ones I hurt, you took my trust for granted, now I'm that malefactor leavin them in the dirt. Painted smiles on my face, but my soul was bruised.
Hurt people hurt people, unwillingly that's the path I chose, wrote verses of pain tryin to find peace but every line I jotted just increased the grief

in this maze of emotions while searchin for light
tryin to heal these wounds, and make it right.

The Power of Choice and Action in Shaping Your Destiny

Every road leads you somewhere, it's up to you to determine what road you take, you control your own burden, you can have light, but if you don't activate it you'll still be in the dark, don't just sit and debate it. Life's a series of choices, paths you must tread, trust in your instincts, let them guide where you're led. Knowledge is power, but it's useless if idle. Action is the key, that's your true survival, you hold the torch, it's your job to ignite the flame of ambition that burns through the night, don't fear the journey, embrace every part. Success is a mindset, it begins in the heart. From the shadows you rise, with your vision so clear, forge your own destiny, let go of the fear.

Each step is a lesson, each fall is a gain in the end, it's your spirit that will always remain.

The Power of Words Behind Bars

The pen was my life line at night time
just sittin in that cell had me outta my
right mind
16 stressed out, feelin' like a dead man
countin' days, thinkin' of the ways I could get a
plan. Paper dreams, they became my escape
route
writin' letters, hopin' someone could hear me
shout.
Walls closin' in, but I had to fight back every
line I wrote kept my soul intact, visions of
freedom danced in my mind's eye.
Bars and steel couldn't crush my will to try
I penned my sorrows, turned pain into prose in
that isolation, my true self arose. Night-
mares and shadows, they haunted my sleep
but in my words, I found strength to keep
pushin' forward, holdin' on to that light the pen
was my weapon in the darkest night.

Prison bars, they couldn't cage my spirit in
every verse, I found a way to live in lines of
hope, they paved my road ahead from those
words, I rose, never feelin' dead. Finally
free, the world now in my hands the pen
and paper was my escape plans I left that
cell, but the lessons stayed with every step, I
walked the path I laid, now I write for those
who can't find their voice
in their silence, I help them make a choice
to believe, to fight, to never give in
for in their stories, new lives can begin..

The Price of Ambition and Loyalty

Late night watchin' Blow, double-crossed times untold, true intentions questionable, like stories grandma told.
Relatin' to George, I can feel his despair, had pockets full once, now nobody cares. Family turned their backs, homeboys switched lanes, thought it was all love, but only received pain. Did my time in a cell, baby mama moved on, came out to nothin' , a decade gone.
And you wonder why Tony killed Manolo, in this world of betrayal, you reap what you sow.
Echoes of the past linger, lessons hard to let go, in the mirror's reflection, scars tell a tale, of loyalty forgotten, where friendships derail.

On to Paid in Full, where the dollars divide,

Mitch's trust in Rico leads to a perilous slide.
Greed fractures bonds once thought to be true,
friendship turns fatal when loyalty's askew.

In Blue Hill Avenue, where friendships twist and bend,
Money's seductive call transforms once-steadfast friends.
A bond forged in laughter, now withers in greed,
as ambition ignites a darkness that's hard to impede.
Once-shared dreams vanish in the shadow of wealth.
The allure of currency eclipses true health.

New Jack City, ambition corrupts the heart,
Nino's own blood becomes a pawn from the start.
Loyalty's lost amidst the hunger to rule,
turnin' close friends into malicious tools.

In The Departed, deception's the game,
partners in crime play with lives and with names.
Smiles hide intent as alliances fray,
in a race for survival, trust withers away.

In Casino, power blinds truth, respect fades,
old friends become foes in ambition's masquerade.
Greed dresses as loyalty, but the mask shatters,
in a world where trust ultimately scatters.

*Under the sun of The Godfather, bloodlines
break,
a family divided by power's cruel stake.
Blood ties torn in pursuit of the crown,
amidst whispers of betrayal, loved ones drown.*

*Training Day paints corruption's cruel stain,
where mentors and allies inflict the most pain.
Even trusted partners can't escape the wrong,
in a world where justice is weak and strings
pull strong.*

*In Scarface, ambition leads a perilous course,
old friends, new enemies, no remorse.
As Tony climbs higher, bonds are estranged,
a cautionary tale of how loyalty's exchanged.*

*Don't forget Snowfall, where Franklin's life's a
dance, caught in a web spun by fortune and
chance.
Cream risin' quick, but it's blood that it stains,
fightin' through danger where trust twists in
chains.
From a kid with a vision, a hustler's ambition.
He built an empire, yet lost his position.
With family close, yet so far away,
friends turned to rivals, a heavy price to pay.
Findin' solace in power, but losin' his way,
every choice a reflection of debt he had to pay.*

*And in Power, where the streets and board-
rooms entwine. Ghost, a master of shadows,
walks a perilous line. Fightin' for freedom,*

but haunted by regret, in a world of ambition, where trust is a threat.
Tommy, loyal yet wild, with a heart forged in flame,
battles his demons, as they stoke his inner shame.
His friendship with Ghost, a bond thick yet frail,
wrestles with betrayal, caught in a ruthless tale.
Ghost's son Tariq, once innocent in gaze,
now stalks the dark alleys, lured by the maze.
Followin' his father into the turmoil and strife,
dancin' with danger, embracin' this new life.
Burdened by legacies, the weight feels severe,
yearnin' for power in a world filled with fear.
Temptation surrounds him, and with each step he takes.
He finds himself tangled in the choices he makes.
Marriages fracture as dark secrets unfold,
whispers of betrayal cut deeper than gold.
Allies twist to rivals, driven by hunger and fame,
in the savage realm of Power, loyalty's aflame.
As ambition devours and shadows loom large,
Tariq walks the path where few return from their charge.
In this fierce landscape, where nothin' remains,
blood ties can fray, and all power strains.

With each movie and show, the stories unfold,
Lives entangled, their secrets retold...

The Quest for Purpose Beyond the Fringes of Life

I often find myself standing at the fringes of society, peering in at the vibrant tapestry of life and the myriad souls that populate it. There are moments when I embark on a solitary journey into the depths of my own existence, wrestling with existential questions that gnaw at my spirit: What is my true direction? What abilities lie dormant within me, waiting to be awakened? What strengths can I draw upon as I navigate this intricate maze we call life? Am I moving toward a profound purpose, or merely hurtling toward the inevitable end, a silent death upon arrival?

(Pause)

Now, that might have sailed over some heads. "Purpose"—the very heartbeat of our existence; the reason for which we embark on this journey. It is life itself, woven with the threads of our unique strengths and abilities. Each of us carries the potential to etch an everlasting imprint on the pages of history. No matter how fleeting our time may be, like so many illustrious figures of the past, our legacies can ripple through the ages, igniting the hopes and dreams of the generations that follow us.

And then there's the haunting notion of "death upon arrival"—are we not all destined for that finality? A staggering portion of humanity drifts through life, tethered to a sense of aimlessness, living in discord with their true selves until they return to the earth, from whence we all came. It is a chilling reminder that while we are here, we must not merely exist; we must strive to thrive, leaving a legacy that defies time.

The Silent Symphony of Emotions

Emotions run deep, like stillwaters unseen.
Feelings surrender to the pulse of our dreams.
With every heartbeat, love's fire redeems,
Igniting our souls, tearing at the seams.
Heartbeats sync with the rhythm of pain,
In life, we lose and we gain.
We chase after happiness but will flee from grief yet in the depths of sorrow we find relief.
Loves gentle whisper, angers fierce roar in a battle of feelings there's always more.
Eyes wide open yet blinded by fear, truth be clear
the heart knows no logic, the mind no peace,
in the war of feelings, there's no quick release..

The Unbreakable Bonds of Friendship

The richest man ain't the one with his first dollar, it's the one still with his first friend, loyalty outlasts fortune, it's a bond that won't bend.
Many people gone walk in and out your life like a transient parade, but only real friends leave footprints on your heart, memories that never fade.
Through thick and thin, they've been your rock, your steady guide in the darkest nights and brightest days, always by your side.
Wealth can't buy that trust, you can't replace that solid bond. It's the comfort in their presence, like the calm of a pond.
A brotherhood of shared dreams, of struggles and of laughs, the richest man knows this well, it's not about the math.
True friends uplift you, they challenge you to grow,

they'll call you out on your flaws, but never let you go.
In a world where money talks it's easy to get lost,
but the value of a true friend, that's beyond any cost.
They'll stand by you in storms and help you weather the gales. Loyalty's unwavering, when all else fails.
So cherish those who stood by, when the world seemed bleak,
They're the ones who see your soul, even when you're weak.
The richest man understands, it's love that truly mends,
It's not about the riches, but the legacy of friends.
As years go by and fortunes change, one thing remains clear,
The measure of a man is the company he keeps near.
The richest man ain't the one with gold stacked to the sky,
It's the one who's loved and cherished, with friends that never say goodbye.

Thinking to Myself

Black-on-Black crime is an issue that must come to a halt somewhere along the way in America, but so too must this unjust killing perpetrated by cops. That doesn't fill me with pride when I say I'm an American, because I'm not. I'll never stand for this country, go to war, or fight for it. I wasn't enslaved for over 400 years, but I can't say the same for some of my peers. Haven't we shed enough blood and held back enough tears? Nah, you bastards won't stop until you commit genocide. Turn the cheek? We should just forget it? No! That doesn't inspire me to say, 'Hey, let's have a million-man march,' because people are doing just that, and still the killings continue, unabated.

I feel everything Meek is spitting in that Instagram post. To understand his reason, you first have to walk in his shoes, endure what he's been through, and witness what he's seen. You know what I mean? I can relate. I'm Black, for one; I'm at the bottom of the barrel, struggling to pave my way to the top. For two, I've had my run-ins with the law. We all make choices in our lives; some just don't get caught for it. Unfortunately, I did.

There's a lot I've seen and witnessed with this so-called justice system we're supposed to rely on for protection. But who do you call when the cops are the ones doing the murdering? All this pain fills me with a hatred for America, deep in my soul. It makes me question the whole theory of this so-called God who is supposed to have made everyone equal. That's a big lie, or I must have missed the memo where they wrote Black lives out. I'm tired of hearing people say, 'It's in God's hands; God will fix it...' When the hell is He or She going to do anything about it? Because Blacks are being taken down like livestock.

Troubled Man

Sometimes the simplest choices lead to the deepest heartaches? inflicted by our own hands or by the love that often breaks.
Lying to myself is nothing but denial's cruel embrace, self-doubt, low self-esteem, a mirror I can't face.
Guilty as charged, I've turned against my own heart,
Let insecurities take the wheel, tearing my world apart.
In relationships, I danced in circles, running back and forth, tarnished trust became the norm, cold comfort of my worth.
I wore a mask, a facade crafted from fear inside,
Never meant to shatter her heart, still I let my secrets slide.
Inconsiderate and cold-hearted, I never meant

to be that man, hiding the truth to shield
her, believing I had a plan.
I thought I was protecting her from the pain
that I foresaw, yet failed to show her the
light that shines even if it's raw.
She didn't lose me; I am the one who let go,
Allowing her to carry burdens that I refused to
show.
All she needed was a hand, a steadying
embrace,
Instead, I stood by like a ghost in an empty
space.
I am just a man, troubled, born into a world of
sin,
didn't choose this winding road, but let the
journey begin.
Each step has left me isolated, exposed, stripped
of my pride, loved her deeply but fumbled,
leaving me empty inside.
I played her heart like a saxophone, the notes a
mournful tune, what spilled out was my
sorrow, a haunting, sad monsoon.
In the echo of my failures, I search for what I've
lost, but the love that could have flourished
came at an unbearable cost.

Truth

Sometimes I pretend, but deep down, I'm flawed. You see, one can act their heart out, but what is it worth if no one applauds? I look around and realize that, for all the wrong reasons, we go hard. I don't own the deed, but I hold the title to that brand-new Benz parked in my front yard. A collection of stainless victims, we are hostages to materialism. We hear and talk about it, point fingers, and watch it on television, yet still fail to grasp the essence. Some of you are deciphering this while others scratch their heads, wondering, 'I don't get it.'

If life were a drug, many of us would be nodding off and throwing up, blissfully oblivious. My ambition fuels my drive; I mean, I want more, but I struggle finding it difficult to go out and seize it. Perhaps I lost you because you think I'm discussing dollar figures, but what I need from you is to pay close attention, not just to the words I'm saying, but to the essence of what I deliver. Don't let me lose you, for then what swirls in your mind will merely become a jumble of gibberish.

What do we live and breathe for? Body kisses between the sheets what do we plant seeds for? Which are you: the one who perceives the point or the one always trying to keep score? Put your mind to it. Some of us just skim through it, trapped in a monotonous routine, waking up and merely breathing, yet refusing to lift a finger while effortlessly regale you with the details of life in HD. Change the channel; it's clear you lack oxygen. Your mind is too wrapped around B.E.T. This is actuality in relation to Trutv.

What flows through my veins is H.History; somewhere along my journey, my ethnicity has been spiked, enabling my mind to transcend the ordinary, a supernatural ticking time bomb, and I don’t mean TNT...

Unbroken Allegiance: Claiming Justice in a Land Struggle

I pledge allegiance to a flag in a country under which I get no justice, the color of my skin is hated and often targeted by cops every day's a struggle, every corner got a plot they see me as a threat, but I'm just trying to survive in a land of broken dreams where only the strong thrive.

The system's rigged, built to keep us down.

They profit off our pain, leave us bleeding on the ground, got me feeling like a pawn in a game I didn't choose.

Every headline's another life we lose marching in the streets, voices rise in the night fighting for a change, but the future's out of sight hands up, don't shoot, but they still let it pop in the shadows of the sirens, our hopes never stop we rise from the ashes, from the pain we were dealt with a fire in our hearts, and the power that we felt bound by our struggle, we refuse to be chained in the land of the free, it's our freedom that we claim.

Unraveling deception and the power of honesty

Why when men don't follow direction it's deception, missteps breed doubt, clouding perception, trust erodes in the wake of deception.

Clarity fades when truth's disregarded, intentions obscured, hearts unguarded. In the maze of miscommunication, love gets lost in misinterpretation. Pride builds walls, creating division, distance grows with every omission.

Transparency's the bridge, yet seldom crossed, in the silence, understanding is lost.

Honesty's the key, though it's often resisted,

without it, bonds become twisted.

The compass of trust points to sincerity, without it, love's a fleeting rarity.

Navigatin' life requires true direction,

deviation leads to heartache and dissection.

Rebuild with truth, let trust be the guide,
deception dies when honesty's applied..

Unshackled

You ever feel blindfolded but your eyes wide open to the world's lies and deceit, but still you hope to be free. I'm caught up in a system where the blind lead the blind searchin' for the truth in a world where deceit intertwined.

Envy will hide behind compliments, be careful who you take 'em from, friends turn foe when the stakes rise, see where they're comin' from it's either that or reap what you sow, snakes don't hiss no more nowadays they call you bro.

Promises made in the dark often fades with the light, chasin' dreams through the struggle, tryin' to get through the night.

The media paints pictures, but they're never quite clear, feedin' us fear while the truth disappears.

Politicians lie for votes, corporations buy their way,
profit over people is the motto they display.
Education's underfunded, prisons overflow,
hope is lost in darkness, where the dreams don't go.
The system is designed to keep us down, but still we grow. In the land of the free, we still fightin' for justice, voices of the voiceless echo, hopin' they trust us. They want us to be silent, but our spirits are loud, unbroken and proud. From Ferguson to Flint, to every hood and block the revolution that's brewin' can't be stopped by a clock.
Economic disparity, the wealth gap is wide,
while the rich keep on risin' , the homeless stay outside.
Healthcare for profit, and the poor ignored,
but we keep pushin' forward, our voices roared.
Racism's a wound that's deep and still bleeds,
generations fightin' for equality's needs,
from Selma to the present, the struggle is alive, in the face of oppression, our spirits revive.
Social media feeds us, but are we being fed?
Likes and shares over substance, what's being said?
Echo chambers traps us in bubbles where we reside,
but breaking free from comfort is where truth can hide.
Mental health's a battle, many men including

myself fight it alone, stigma keeps us silent,
but we're not on our own.
Our history is written in the blood of the
brave,
those who stood for justice, even when
enslaved.
From Harriet, Malcom, Huey to Martin, June-
teenth is their legacy we hold. In every act
of courage, our stories unfold.
Equality and justice, the fight is far from done,
but through unity and action, the battle
can be won.
Our voices are powerful, our cause is just, keep
the buck in ourselves and each other, we
place our trust...

Using Sex to Heal

Sometimes as men, we use sex as a tool to rid ourselves of pain, drownin' in the flesh to try and wash off the stain. Broken inside, but the mask stays the same, in a room full of bodies, but alone inside our brain.
Chasin' release, but it never quite sticks, each moment of pleasure's a temporary fix.
Intimacy's hollow, just a physical act, a fleeting escape then feelin' detached, and the cycle just continues, emotions react but we're always pulled back.
Numb to the core, but the need's ever-present, our thoughts become crescent, the truth's omnipresent,
sex as our solace, but the solace is transient.
We use it to forget, to silence the ache,
to fill the abyss, every kiss that we take,
deep down we know, it's a bitter heartbreak,
temporary pleasure, a soul we forsake.

We pretend it's control, we pretend it's a shield,
a battlefield of sheets, where our scars are concealed, but the duel's internal, in the darkness revealed, in the act of escape, our true selves we wield.
Yet, in the end we're just runnin' from pain,
lost in the motion, tryin' to sustain,
but the emptiness lingers, a hauntin' abstain.
Sometimes as men, we use sex to sustain.
In moments of passion, we misplace our trust, but the morning reminds us, we're left in disgust.
hidin' from demons, in a bed full of lust,
Connections are ephemeral, our touch turns to dust.
Just a silhouette in the rain drownin' in trauma, loneliness and abandonment, emptiness has us searchin' for a way to feel sane.

Voice's

Vagrant thoughts pierce my mind, an unrelenting force that seeks direction, burrowing deep into my cranium without a hint of tranquility. They yearn for freedom, longing to escape and roam wild, but they are trapped—nowhere to vanish, to run, or to hide. Instantly, they meld into a cacophony of incoherent voices inside my head, layers upon layers of tumultuous thoughts pulling me unnervingly in every direction but one. The brutal grip of lies and deceit confronts me like a raging bull, suspended in a precarious balance, like a noose tightening around my psyche.

These voices echo within me, resembling Cole Sear but conjuring no Sixth Sense; I don't hear the dead. Instead, I hear the whispers of betrayal, each discouragement, every insidious lie, the stark reality of abandonment—these are my ghosts.

War is the front line, a brutal ballet of chaos
where combat erupts at point-blank range,
leaving adversaries' brains exposed like a
scene from Mars Attacks, war is that grim
reality of America's relentless assaults on
Iraq.

War is an atmosphere heavy with silence, it
looms larger and feels more menacing than
any spoken threat. In the shadow of
conflict, silence becomes the only strategy,
the only way to tread forward.

War is bloodshed, a symphony of gunfire and
the clatter of shell casings, knives glinting
under a blood-red sky, anything, any
instrument of destruction, wielded to usher
in demise. There's no resolution, no peace
talks, only a grim ledger of obituaries and
bodies outlined in stark white chalk.

War is the jarring lack of sleep behind enemy

lines, a heightened paranoia that churns in your gut, the heart-stopping fear that at any moment, you could lose your life to the chaos of conflict, that bitter beef.

In war, the strong dominate the weak, while the wise orchestrate the moves of the strong. To survive, one must know their adversary inside and out, an unrelenting mental game. Fas est ab hoste doceri—a reminder that it is not just right, but essential to learn from one's enemy.

Warrant

A man is only as good as the fruits he chooses to consume, if his mind is wrapped in greed, pride, lust, anger, and gloom. Then those toxic traits seep through, staining his very core, transforming his spirit, leaving his outlook bleak and sore.
A heart filled with envy and sloth breeds instability's strife, his essence dimmed, lost in shadows, a tumultuous life.
But a man with clarity, focus, and discipline to guide,
Is a powerhouse of strength, where true greatness won't hide.
He's a profound thinker, crafting plans in hushed reverie,
Plotting quietly, building dreams, letting his vision run free.
Nothing in this world can match his deeply held ties, To family, life, love, loyalty,

honesty, his guiding skies. Wisdom weaves through his existence, a tapestry of grace, Each attribute a reflection of the light he's proud to embrace. In the garden of his soul, these values bloom and thrive, making him not just a man, but a beacon, truly alive.

Weight of a Fatherless Journey

I look in the mirror and it's a reflection of what I've heard people made my features grow into. That's why I stay away from family because I'm constantly reminded of how much I look like you. I can't call you my pops nor father, you're just a man, a stranger I never knew. Growing up my brothers had fathers so did my auntie Rachel. Abusive household alone I wasn't introduced to another side of the family to run to, how do you think that made me feel when you lived in the same town but never never considered to come through. Here I grew no words of advice, no warm embrace, not even a I love you. A lot of things I had to teach myself without you. During my child-hood days not knowing l only heard about you, in all reality you were a good man from what I learned but for you to spit me out then go and lace up your running shoes did I deserve that?. I was just a baby, what could I have possibly done to you for you to look at me as yesterday's paper, old news. Do you remember the one time we were introduced that day you bought me a 20 ounce soda and made a promise as to what you'd do. I never saw that bike but what I did get is that feeling of being lied to. Mama used to tell me you wasn't shit I ain't believe her though until our next encounter my depiction of you made an unimaginable emotion unfold, feels like yesterday I was 12 years old for you to be absent all those years over hearing you discuss discipline, saying you'd do something to me that shit turned me cold, you ain't even know me so how was I someone you could say you'd put your hands on. Wasn't in your company for no more than two weeks and even though you never said it directly to me, with a stare that could pierce the soul I told you I was ready to go home, the entire ride was silent, at the bus station you could at least told me, let me know if you make it home. But there was nothing. I exited your truck feeling like the kid father by Karl Malone. When you broke the opportunity never presents itself to be a shareholder so I used EBT to buy this chip on my shoulder. All those years I lived with animosity I shouldn't have had, how could I allow someone who's never been in my life to have such an effect over me emotionally in that moment I rose from the ashes with two options get angry or get in my feet like a drug addict fighting an addiction telling themselves, I choose me. So as I think about my own kids and though I no longer have questions nor do the thoughts as to what I said if we ever speak cross my mind, I don't view you as a deadbeat in your absence you taught me how to be. Be present, be loving, be caring and encouraging. Being there when the world seems like it's too much to bear my kids will always know their fathers here.

What I lived through

Lately, I've been going through the same thing; the stress from struggling makes it hard to remain sane. What do you do when you're down on your luck, hurting bad? Imagine spending your last few dollars on gas, turning around only to have your ride impounded for outdated tags. Then, you make it to work late, and they let you go, just for you to walk home and find an eviction notice waiting for you.

Feels like yesterday not just a couple of years ago I was sitting in a cell, fighting demons and losing hope. Piss-poor, gambling with my life over a bar of soap. Stressed out, riots on the yard got me thinking: Will I make it to see another 24? I've been talking to God, but I don't think he listening though all that praying ever did was leave me with a strep throat. So I'm walking with the devil, ready to go toe to toe with the warden or the C.O., so I don't ask why, at least not anymore.

I'm from a land of no sanity, no belief, no hope. All you get is government assistance, a church, and a liquor store.

That same soap I was gambling my life for? I've seen a dude put it in a sock his weapon. Nine months in the hole had me losing weight. Lord, I just want to live it up, and we just want to live and that's something you should know. Growing up, sheets and blankets that's hardwood. I slept on the floor. Can you imagine what it's like being broke, putting your feet in a pair of shoes your brother wore about a year ago? Or eating the same meal as the day before? Some will rob, steal, or kill just to get that dough.

I watched my mom use it, so I converted to selling that dope. Once an innocent kid, it's funny but the way I've been feeling, I'd hog-tie Diddy for a piece of that dirty money. I came home after almost ten years, and it was clear these people didn't have anything for me. Yeah, they smiled and welcomed me back, but I won't say nothing. When I was in that cell, a piece of mail, a phone call, or a visit? I didn't see none of that.

COGNIZANT THINKIN'

What if Malcolm X had been a Christian and had white skin? What if his reasoning about the Bible held the same weight as his views on Islam?

What if Martin Luther King Jr. were the Grand Wizard of the Ku Klux Klan? Would he have received more recognition than just a single commemorative day, or would he still be alive today to witness the fulfillment of his dream?

What if there existed a free cure for AIDS, with death stemming only from a lack of knowledge about self-improvement or the natural process of aging?

What if George W. Bush really didn't care for Black people, and when confronted about

it, he expressed no shame? And what if our first Black president, Barack Obama, was a Muslim with ties to Saddam Hussein?
I once heard a white man say that Christianity was a religion created by and for white people. That perspective isn't too far from the truth. What if, during slavery, Europeans commandeered our religion and forced us into submissive Christianity, despite speculation that the Black race was foundational to Islam before the abduction of Black men and women?

What if the Willie Lynch Letter was actually authored by a Black man, outlining strategies for the oppression of Europeans?
What if, for every white person, three Black individuals were wealthy?

What if Black judges wrongfully convicted whites without guilt, while Black police officers were acquitted for acts of vigilantism against whites? This notion of America as the "land of the free" eludes me. America was built on my blood, sweat, tears, and sacrifices, so why are laws consistently set against me?
Why do we perpetuate lies when there's a scripture in the Bible that states, "The truth will set you free"? Free from what? The eternal consequences of our repeated sins? Here on Earth, the justice system seems solely focused on infinite currency.

What if schools taught Black students the full potential of their cultural history instead of a watered-down version of the truth? Why do we pay taxes if there's no genuine investment in education?

What if racism had never existed? Perhaps, then, I would never have been exposed to the thoughts and realizations that shape my perspective today.

Where I'm From

I exist in a society where the innocent minds of babies are plucked away, abortion after abortion—a grim reality in which women, with a twisted sort of pride, mimic Brenda, tossing infants into dumpsters without a second thought. I inhabit a society where this tragedy is recorded on greenbacks, emblazoned with "In God We Trust," all while a sinister force reigns unchallenged over us. It's a bitter truth: we the people are crumbling, suffering under the weight of mental anguish, living like reckless fools. The absence of wisdom leaves us bereft, with nothing to show for our struggles. A man just returned home on parole, still hiding his stash, wrapped in the swirling haze of molly, weed, and crack smoke that has suffocated our community, far more damaging than any political candidate could ever be.

State assistance keeps women entrenched in ignorance. Each day, I stride through life as if tomorrow might never dawn, refusing to let comfort settle in. Instead, I ace each trial as it comes, aware that the moment we think we're gliding along smoothly, the incline of reality kicks in, throwing us into a daunting uphill battle. We find ourselves window shopping in life's bazaar, hesitant to reach for a higher plane, oblivious to the future lurking ahead. In our doubt, we unwittingly sabotage our own destinies.

Whispers of Regret:

A FATHER'S LETTER FROM CONFINEMENT

In the quiet confinement of my cell, I pen these
words with a heavy heart full of pain.
Ten years slipped through like grains of sand,
moments I missed, too many to understand.
I think of your first day of school, your little
backpack, your face with a huge smile
shining through. Instead of writing this
letter full of regret I should have been there
for you.
While you waved goodbye with a heart full of
dreams, I was lost in a world where hopes
kept under wrap and often unseen.
I was left only imagining the echoes of laughter
on a sunlit street, as you learned to ride,
two wheels at your feet.
I can see you wobbling, then soaring high,
but I wasn't there, just a whisper unheard from
the inside.
Your first little trophies, gleaming bright,

the games that you played, the passion you
possess and the toughness in your fight.
Each score that you made, every cheer from the
crowd, I missed it all and for that my
heart's heavy, unbowed.
I think of the nights when you'd search for a
hand,
some comfort, some guidance, a love that could
stand. I long to protect you, to show you I
care,
but time took me far it left us lost in despair.
I missed your first steps, the milestones you
sought,
while the years of solitary confinement
consumed me, with lessons untaught.
I wanted to guide you through struggles and
fears,
but all I could offer were silent aching tears.
I see the man that you've come to be, a father
and leader, with strength flowing free.
You took every lesson, every hardship and
pain,
and built up your life like the sun after it rains.
I hope you forgive me though I'll never be the
same. If I could wish for anything it would
be fix the things that to day that makes me
ashamed.
My absence was a lesson etched deep inside my
heart, a reminder that love can't be torn
apart, through years of separation, the
distance and the pain, my love for you is a
constant never ending gain.
My firstborn, my pride and my son from the

depths of my heart, I cherish everyday,
you're the light and strength in my life in
every way.
Though years may have passed, and the road
has been long, I'm by your side to continue
to help you grow stronger for the man
you've become. I'm honored to say, I love
you and I'm grateful for you each and
everyday.

Whispers to My Past:

A JOURNEY FROM SHADOWS TO TRUE CONNECTION

To you, my past self, who once believed, I yearn for moments steeped in understandin', where conversations flow like rivers, deep and true. The kind of exchange that ignites smiles with memories of what was and dreams of what could be, escapin' the shadows of empty phrases like, "You know what I'm sayin'?"

In those lingerin' nights, we'd pause our talks only for love's embrace—intimate and unrelentin'. We'd cherish the profound art of truly knowin' one another, transcendin' the mundane with words that dance beyond life's horizon. The joy of whisperin' "I love you" would be eternal, its passion undyin'.

Pride would grow in the companionship of a soul revealed—jointly fuellin' the flames of endless commitment. Mutual effort—a pledge inscribed on every heart. Mutual. Let it echo within every conscience.

Yet, I wonder now, did I wander astray in my quest for love's truth? The light of realization was dimmed, revealin' the chill of love's facade. I've danced in no-strings-attached soirées, fooling the heart. But there is always that string, woven with discovery, entanglin' life itself.

On one end, a selfish heart might play puppet master, manipulatin' dreams like a schemin' figure who delights in takin' more than she gives. I, too, once optimistic, became ensnared in such games, veering toward loneliness by choice.

Yet still, I write to you, hoping to find love anew.

5/13/09

Why 3 Peat

Why is the blood that runs through my veins blue, we make movies and speculate but what if the aliens we speak of were actually me and you. We talk about life on other planets and if it's true W.W.C.C.D. You don't have to ask what would Christopher Columbus would do.

Why do Russia have it out for Ukraine at one point in history before 1991 amongst the two it was all love so why beef with one another when so much can be accomplished when everyone's on the same page. Why is America always quick to run to someone else's aid but won't engage in the problems on their own front page. Here it is 2023 the prison system is still overcrowded with blacks, it was televised while on his stomach a cop pulled his gun and shot an unarmed man in the back. ...what if the irs was ran by blks

1/18/23

Why2

Yo, how in 2017 they let Trump buy the
election?
Wanna build a wall, but the problem's bigger
than a Mexican.
16 women with allegations, Cosby tried to own
a network, but now he's locked up for the
same transgression, isn't that suspect?
Turn the other cheek, ‘cause they bought the
election?
Every election year it's the same old story:
A Black man's killed, a mass shooting, or a kid
with a gun at school, it's all so gory.
Starting to feel like it's performative, orches-
trated pain. America‘s drowning deep in
deception's chains. A Black man says
slavery was a choice, wears that red hat
with pride,
"Make America Great Again" while we still
face racism outside.

Why every time I turn on the news, it's another
Black body shot down,
It's not just sad anymore; it's a sickening,
constant sound.
What if Trump, start The First Purge?
I'm making a hit list, Crooked cops, judges,
prosecutors—they won't be missed.
For centuries, Black kids witness the cycle of
pain,
Innocence lost, living in a world that's insane.
Drug rates soaring, homeless kids on the street.
Cops killing, reverting to brutality, a
reality we can't defeat. Politicians lie, keep
the people blind, corporate interests and
greed, they've lost their mind demonizin
the poor, but praise the wealthy few.
Why is it that this country always turns a blind
eye to the truth? It's nothing new
We scream for change, but they ignore the cries
media distorts, feeding us with lies, divide
and conquer, is their master plan pittin us
against each other, man against man.
Incarceration nation, prisons overflowing with
systemic racism, the evidence is showing.
Gun violence rampant, yet they stall on
laws profiting from chaos, ignoring the
flaws.
We march in protest, but they quell the fight
with tear gas and batons, suppressing our right
to speak, to live, to dream and to be free in this
land of the brave, home of hypocrisy but
still we rise, we resist, we won't be tamed
fighting for justice, we won't be shamed.

For every life lost, for every tear shed,
We must stand united, our spirits never dead.
Change is coming, it's on the horizon.
Through the pain and struggle, we keep our eyes
On a better future, where truth will reign.
Until then, we endure, breaking every chain.

About the Author

I was born in Michigan, specifically in a small town called Benton Harbor. As the youngest of three boys, I faced significant challenges, enduring neglect and both physical and mental abuse from a young age. During our mother's time in prison, my siblings and I were raised by our grandmother in the Vineyard projects a place notorious for its harsh conditions in the early 90s. It would be an understatement to say we didn't witness and experience things that would leave any child traumatized. On top of this, we also faced abuse from our grandmother, which made our situation even more difficult.

My oldest brother eventually ran away, and my other brother had his father for support, but I felt utterly alone. By the mid-90s, our mother was released from prison, and we moved to Grand Rapids, a city that operated at a much faster pace than our previous home. Over the years, very little changed. Our mother remained emotionally and morally absent, forcing us to navigate our own lives. As a child left to make crucial decisions alone, the conclusions I reached were often drastic, shaped by the difficult circumstances I faced.

By the age of 14, I became a father for the first time. Just a year later, I was expelled from high school after getting into a fight as an act of self-defense. Suddenly, I found myself on my own, struggling to navigate adulthood. At that age, I couldn't find a job and didn't even know my social security number. But, despite these challenges, I had a child to care for. I turned to what I had known my entire life for survival, the streets.

Just when I thought things couldn't get any worse, at the age of 16, I was incarcerated. I lost a decade of my life not willingly, but as a result of my struggles with self-discipline. Anger consumed me, and I often felt isolated; I had no one to turn to, leading to a sense of being invisible. I didn't know how to process my emotions, which ultimately resulted in me spending an entire year in solitary confinement. In that confined space, I began to reflect on my life. During that year, I took it upon myself to learn how to read and write. I've always been a fan of rap music, drawn to how artists articulate their lives through words. Inspired by this, I started writing my own thoughts and feelings down. Writing became my escape, a powerful means to channel my pain into something meaningful. It liberated me from the chains of my past and everything that had held me captive throughout my life. This transformative journey through writing is how my second book, *Beauty and the Bastard*, came to be.

www.ingramcontent.com/pod-product-compliance
Lightning Source LLC
LaVergne TN
LVHW010051170826
845678LV00012B/2106

* 9 7 9 8 8 9 5 6 9 9 9 0 4 *